DATE DUE

THE EURO-BOND MARKET

By the same author

The Euro-Dollar System: Practice and Theory of
International Interest Rates

The History of Foreign Exchange

A Dynamic Theory of Forward Exchange

Foreign Exchange Crises

A Textbook on Foreign Exchange

Leads and Lags: The Main Cause of Devaluation

Decline and Fall? Britain's Crisis in the Sixties

THE
EURO-BOND
MARKET

PAUL EINZIG

*Progress in improving the free world's capital
markets has become essential if the uninhibited
flow of long-term international portfolio capital
is not to be a disturbing element in the quest for
payments equilibrium.*
Douglas Dillon, Secretary of the
U.S. Treasury, 1961–64

MACMILLAN

ST MARTIN'S PRESS

First Edition (published under the title of Foreign Dollar Loans in Europe) 1965
Second Edition (extensively revised and enlarged) 1969

Published by
MACMILLAN AND CO LTD
Little Essex Street London W C 2
and also at Bombay Calcutta and Madras
Macmillan South Africa (Publishers) Pty Ltd Johannesburg
The Macmillan Company of Australia Pty Ltd Melbourne
The Macmillan Company of Canada Ltd Toronto
St Martin's Press Inc New York
Gill and Macmillan Ltd Dublin

Library of Congress catalog card no. 70–83202

Printed in Great Britain by
R. & R. CLARK LTD
Edinburgh

Contents

Preface to the Second Edition

THE spectacular expansion of the European market in foreign bonds since the publication of the first edition of this book five years ago has amply confirmed my confidence in its prospects. At that time this market was all but universally regarded as a mere temporary expedient serving the purpose of overcoming a passing difficulty. The adverse balance of payments of the United States called for efforts to divert from New York to Europe the demand for long-term capital which until then was met by issues of foreign loans by American banks. It had been assumed that once the balance of payments deficit was brought under control, New York would resume its former rôle.

Today it is the unanimous opinion of banking circles and official circles alike on both sides of the Atlantic that the European market for foreign bonds, which barely existed in 1964, has become an important and permanent integral part of the international financial system. Indeed it is widely assumed that there is ample scope for its further expansion.

Apart altogether from the increased importance of the market and from the recognition of its permanent character, it witnessed during the past five years several institutional changes which have considerably altered its character. Originally its activities consisted almost entirely in the issue of conventional bonds, mostly for foreign Governments or other official borrowers. Today the majority of its issues consist of convertible debentures of business corporations.

Another important though possibly temporary change is that the United States has become the principal foreign borrower in Europe. Further, although most bonds are still issued in terms of dollars, a noteworthy and increasing proportion is now issued in D. marks. It is no longer virtually exclusively a dollar bond market, which is one of the reasons why it has come to be known under the name of the 'Euro-bond market'. Hence the change of the title of this revised edition of my book.

Nevertheless, the large majority of issues continues to be in terms of dollars. For this reason, in spite of the growing importance of Euro-bond issues in terms of D. marks and, to a less extent, in terms of composite units of account, I feel still justified in treating the subject essentially from the angle of a market in dollar bonds. The majority of chapters refer only casually to bonds in other units, in order to avoid complicating further a subject which is already sufficiently involved if one tries to follow up its manifold ramifications.

I sought to do justice, however, to the increased importance of D. mark issues and of West Germany's increased importance as a lender, by devoting a separate chapter to this aspect of the subject. Other new chapters in this edition deal with convertible bonds, with American borrowing, with trends in Euro-bond prices, and with the highly developed secondary market which had barely existed when the original edition of this book was written.

Another sphere in which there were extensive changes since the publication of the book was in exchange control regulations which were tightened considerably. The chapter on investment dollars had to be rewritten to describe these changes and their effects on activities in the market.

I should like to take this opportunity for an earnest appeal to bankers, financial editors, economists and others interested in the European market for dollar bonds to abstain from confusing that market with the Euro-dollar market. It is utterly wrong to call Euro-bonds Euro-dollars. They are two totally different devices. Euro-dollars are dollar deposits re-lent by holders resident outside the United States. They differ fundamentally from dollar bonds issued in Europe, which should be called 'Euro-bonds' or 'Euro-issues' – a term which conveniently covers also bonds issued in currencies other than dollars.

To my mind the loose application of the term 'Euro-dollars' with reference to medium- and long-term bonds has created fully as much confusion in the sphere of international finance as did the inexplicable and illogical war-time change of the name of the Near East to 'Middle East' in the sphere of geography.

I am greatly indebted to a large number of active operators in the Euro-bond market and in the market in investment currencies for their generous assistance in my task to bring my book up to date. Likewise, I am grateful to British and American official quarters for their explanation and interpretation of the changes in the regulations affecting both markets.

P. E.

120 CLIFFORD'S INN,
LONDON, E.C.4
February 1969

A 2

Preface to the First Edition

IT is always a fascinating experience to observe how institutional changes come about, and our post-war generation has been fortunate in having lived through that experience in generous measure in the international financial sphere. During the 'fifties and 'sixties new systems, devices and methods have come into existence in that sphere before our very eyes, in answer to challenges offered by difficult and even apparently insoluble problems.

The institutional change which this book aims at describing and analysing is at the time of writing still at a relatively early phase of its evolution. Although a large number of dollar loans were issued in London in 1963–64, and in Continental centres during the late 'fifties and early 'sixties, their volume has not been sufficiently large so far to constitute a factor of an importance comparable to that of the Euro-dollar system – the lending of short- and medium-term dollar deposits in Europe. Quite conceivably the development of the system of issuing long-term dollar bonds in European markets will follow a course similar to that followed by the development of the Euro-dollar market which, ever since its experimental beginnings in 1957, has been expanding almost uninterruptedly until it became a major factor in foreign exchange markets and money markets. It may take, however, some time before the system of European long-term dollar loans could attain a comparable influence.

I am convinced that even if the expansion of the system of issuing dollar bonds, or any foreign bonds in terms of currencies other than that of the country in which they are issued, should be interrupted by some major reverse – as indeed it might well be sooner or later – in the long run it would resume its progress, in the same way as the Euro-dollar system resumed it after each setback. Now that the world of international finance has become familiar with both systems, they are likely to remain an integral part of the international financial mechanism. The change which the advent of the system of issuing dollar bonds outside the United States has brought about is in keeping with the basic trend pointing towards an increasing internationalisation of finance.

Possibly the dollar may not always retain its present prominence as the favourite currency of foreign loan contracts chosen for such transactions in Europe. In fact there have been many loans issued in other foreign currencies and in composite units of account, and these loans have played a part similar to that of European dollar loans, albeit to a lesser degree. But just as Euro-dollars overshadow, and are likely to continue to overshadow in the long run, all other Euro-currencies, so these European dollar bonds are, and are likely to remain in the long run, more important than foreign bonds issued in Europe in other foreign currencies. In any case the operation of the system is substantially the same whether the currency of the loan contracts is the dollar, or some other hard currency, or a composite unit of account, so long as it is not the local currency of the capital market in which the loans are issued. For this reason, our findings could be adapted, with relatively little modification, to a system under which some other currency unit would have for some time at any rate the same prominence as the dollar has at the time of writing.

When the Euro-dollar system drifted into existence during 1957–59 it escaped for a long time the attention of financial commentators (including myself). That history had not repeated itself, and could not possibly repeat itself, in respect of European dollar bonds. From the very outset there was bound to be much more publicity about such transactions than there was until comparatively recently about Euro-dollars. This is only natural. The Euro-dollar market was for years hidden from economists and other readers of the financial Press by a remarkable conspiracy of silence. Bankers deliberately avoided discussing it with financial editors, presumably for fear that publicity might attract additional rivals to the market, or that it might breed criticism in the Press and opposition in official quarters. I stumbled on its existence by sheer accident in October 1959 – having overlooked, I must confess frankly, a brief article on the subject that appeared in the *Economist* some months earlier – and when I embarked on an inquiry about it in London banking circles several bankers emphatically asked me not to write about the new practice, except perhaps in articles in learned journals or in my books which, they assumed, were in any case too technical for the uninitiated. But it would not have been possible to try to conceal in a similar way dollar bond issues from the wider public. Lending and borrowing of dollar deposits is arranged between foreign exchange departments of banks and foreign exchange brokers on their private telephone lines, with a complete exclusion of publicity. Public issues of bonds, on the other hand, by their very nature, have to be advertised in the Press even if they are not offered for subscription to the general public, and they are necessarily commented upon extensively in the financial columns.

It took something like three years before the Euro-dollar market came to be noticed at all, and even today it does not receive anything like the attention it deserves. It took a further three years before the Central Banks primarily concerned with the practice came to initiate a much-needed exhaustive inquiry, through the medium of the Bank for International Settlements, to ascertain the relevant facts and figures and to analyse their broader implications. Even now, some seven years after dealings in Euro-dollars first became a factor of importance, there is usually a time-lag between changes in the practice and their realisation outside the circle of those directly concerned. And such quotations of Euro-dollar rates as appear in the Press only indicate approximate levels of the rates, not the actual rates at which transactions take place in inter-bank dealings.

On the other hand, facts and figures relating to the practice of issuing foreign dollar loans in Britain and on the Continent are necessarily published in the prospectuses of these issues. Their terms – interest rates, issue prices, redemption dates, etc.

– have to be publicised to comply with regulations, even if the whole amounts of the issues had been placed privately in advance of the publication of the prospectuses. The bonds are quoted on Stock Exchanges, even if dealings in them are relatively infrequent. There is a fair amount of current comment on such issues in the financial Press, but they are examined mainly from the point of view of their attractiveness as investments. Admittedly, from time to time financial editors comment on them also from a general technical or economic angle and some of their articles are profound and penetrating. Even so, many fine points of practical or theoretical importance have not been adequately explored, or their position in the system as a whole has not been made clear. Up to the time of writing there has been no systematic attempt – apart from the Report of the U.S. Treasury, *A Description and Analysis of Certain European Capital Markets*, which is largely confined to fact-finding – to present a complete picture of the system and its manifold impact on the national and international economy.

The object of this book is partly to provide factual material and partly to call the attention of economists and of practical experts to the broader implications of the system it describes. I also endeavour to cover two systems closely related to the issue of European dollar bonds – the system of investment dollars and that of composite units of account. I feel that the space devoted to these subjects calls for no apology.

The change of Government in Britain in October 1964 has introduced an element of uncertainty about the prospects of the market for European dollar bond issues, at any rate as far as London is concerned. Up to the time of writing the new Government has not indicated any intention to adopt exchange restrictions of a kind that would interfere with London's rôle as an entrepôt for foreign capital. But the possibility of such measures cannot be ruled out. Although the placing of foreign bonds with non-resident investors, or even with U.K. investors wishing to replace their existing foreign investments, does not impose any additional burden on the balance of payments, many Socialists are opposed to the practice on the ground of their ideological objections to the maintenance of London's rôle as an international banking centre. They are in favour of relinquishing that rôle because of fears that its fulfilment is liable to conflict with the interests of an expansionary domestic economic policy.

Be that as it may, it must be realised that Britain is not in a position to relinquish that rôle. If my banker did not like my account he could close it by sending me a banker's draft to repay my balance. But how could London repay foreign balances amounting to thousands of millions of pounds out of its dwindling gold reserve that could not be sufficient to cover a fraction of those balances? It is obviously impossible. The large size of foreign holdings of sterling compels London to continue to play the part of a world banker, whether we like it or not. And, that being so, it is to our interest to play that part efficiently. The new device described in this book has contributed towards making London's international banking mechanism more efficient, and for that reason alone it would be a pity to destroy it. But the issuing of foreign dollar bonds through London is well worth maintaining also for the sake of the invisible exports it yields, directly and indirectly, to this country.

In addition to studying the existing literature on the subject, contained mostly in official reports and in financial columns, I endeavoured to ascertain the relevant facts and their interpretations by means of direct inquiries from issuing houses and Stock Exchange firms which are engaged in such transactions mainly in London but also in other financial centres. I sought to obtain the benefit of the views of practical experts on the significance, advantages and disadvantages, limitations and prospects of the new system. I am indeed very much indebted for their generous assistance. Since, however, interpretations and even factual information obtained from various equally authoritative quarters were often contradictory – an experience explained by the fact that no individual, however active, is in a position to have direct knowledge of more than a fraction of the total activity – I had to rely largely on my own judgement when deciding which of the conflicting facts or views I should adopt. Responsibility for my findings is, therefore, entirely my own, and I have no wish to pass on any part of it to those who had helped me, by resorting to the all-too-familiar device of mentioning their names, thereby using their recognised authority for endorsing by implication my statements of fact and my opinions, in spite of disclaiming any intention to do so.

P. E.

120 CLIFFORD'S INN,
LONDON, E.C.4
November 1964

CHAPTER ONE

Introduction

THERE is hardly anything new under the sun. Almost every institution, within and without the sphere of the economic system, can be traced to have existed in earlier times, at any rate in some rudimentary form. There are, of course, any numbers of precedents for dollar loans issued outside the United States before 1914, and again during the inter-war period. Nevertheless, I feel justified in regarding the sudden expansion of the practice of issuing such loans during 1963–1969 as an innovation in the same sense as the acceleration in automation or the expansion of hire-purchase after the second World War were institutional developments of importance in spite of the existence of both systems in earlier periods.

The device of re-depositing dollars outside the United States, too, had existed long before the late 'fifties, but this fact does not affect the revolutionary character of the institutional change caused by the spectacular expansion of the Euro-dollar system in recent years. Likewise, the emergence of a European market for foreign dollar bonds has opened a new chapter in the long history of international capital transactions. Such capital movements have a very extensive literature, and the present volume is confined to one of their special aspects – the issuing of foreign loans in Europe in terms of U.S. dollars or in terms of currencies inspiring confidence among investors in countries where they are issued. It is not concerned with direct investment abroad, or with portfolio investment abroad in the form of equities, or with short-term credit transactions unless they arise from medium- or long-term foreign loans in Europe. There is no rigid line of demarcation between international money market and international capital market. It would be idle to try to lay down a firm rule about the length of maturity beyond which a loan transaction becomes a capital transaction. The rule adopted by the United States Treasury in its Report on *A Description and Analysis of Certain European Capital Markets*, that any transaction beyond twelve months constitutes a capital transaction, is not shared either by practical experts or by economists. Even the more popular textbook-rule, that credits up to twelve months are short-term transactions, from one to five years medium-term transactions and over five years long-term transactions, is open to question.

A more acceptable rule is that, broadly speaking, the international money market is concerned with self-liquidating current transactions while the international capital market is concerned with foreign financing of capital expenditure. In practice there can be, however, no clear-cut distinction on such lines. Long-term capital is often borrowed to meet requirements of working capital for the purpose of financing current transactions – even governments often issue long-term bonds abroad to meet current budgetary deficits – while short-term credits are often used, by means of repeated renewal, for financing capital expenditure. For our purpose the criterion is whether funds are raised by means of obtaining some form of bank credit or by issuing long-term securities.

Loans to foreign borrowers are usually granted in terms of the lending country's currency. This is only natural. A lending country's currency is almost invariably harder than a borrowing country's currency. A borrower would not find it easy to obtain accommodation if he insisted on borrowing in his own currency, or at any rate the terms on which he might obtain such loans would necessarily be costly. To investors in the lending country loans in the borrowing country's currency would appear unattractive and adequate response to the issue could only be secured by offering a higher yield. Since demand for foreign loans almost always exceeds the amount of capital readily available for that purpose lenders hold most of the trumps, so that they are usually in a position to insist on bonds in the demonination of their own currency or some other currency (or combination of currencies) that suits their convenience.

Before the war when some international loans were issued simultaneously in more than one lender country each tranche was usually made in terms of the currency of the country in which it was issued, In some instances these tranches were interchangeable and the bonds were in fact shifted frequently from one country to another through stock arbitrage. Creditors had sometimes the advantage of an option clause under which they were entitled to claim payment of principal and interest in the currency of any of the countries in which they were paying agents for the loan. In many other instances foreign loan contracts included a gold clause guaranteeing the gold value of the payments.

During the 19th century many United States loans were issued in Europe in terms of dollars. In the inter-war period Holland and Switzerland were willing to participate in international loans issued in terms of dollars or sterling. Moreover, substantial blocks of many European dollar loans issued in New York were usually placed privately in various European markets – not least in London – during periods when public issues of foreign bonds in terms of dollars were under an unofficial but effective ban. In addition, a large proportion of foreign loans issued in New York and originally placed in the United States had the habit of finding their way back gradually to the borrowing countries or to other European countries.

The main difference between these precedents and the present practice of issuing dollar loans largely in Europe lies in the very large proportion of the total foreign borrowing that assumes the latter form. Instead of being occasional transactions, the issue of dollar bonds in Europe has become the prevalent practice. In the past dollar loans finding their way to Britain constituted a mere fraction of foreign loans issued in London in terms of sterling. The same was true more or less about other European markets. From the late 'fifties, however, a very high proportion of bond issues in Europe came to assume the form of dollar bonds. From the middle 'sixties, even U.S.

borrowing came to assume increasingly that form. In the late 'sixties an increasing minority of Euro-issues came to assume the form of D. mark bonds.

There can be no doubt that issues of Euro-bonds – the name under which these issues have come to be known – have assumed sufficiently large proportions to make it necessary to envisage them as a factor liable to affect foreign exchange markets and money markets in a way that differs in some essential respects from the effects of foreign issues made in terms of the currencies of countries where they are issued. In one actual instance the new device played a decisive part – in 1968 it balanced the payments deficit of the United States. Its expansion has confronted those in charge of monetary policy in general, and foreign exchange policy in particular, with a new set of problems,

Up to now the specific effect of Euro-bond issues, as distinct from the general effects of lending and borrowing abroad, have not yet become sufficiently evident to enable us to reach any definite conclusion about the broader problems involved. The present analysis of the system is bound to be, therefore, largely provisional, subject to revision in the light of subsequent experience and of its closer analysis.

Our first step is to study the background to the development of the new practice. In the next chapter an attempt is made to list the requirements of a good capital market in general and the specific requirements of a good capital market for foreign loans in particular. Such a preliminary survey is essential in order to enable us to appreciate the significance of the changes that have made it necessary to expand the practice of issuing loans in terms of a foreign currency. Chapter 3 describes the extent to which the requirements of good capital markets, as defined in Chapter 2, had existed before the first World War and also during the inter-war period, while Chapter 4 indicates the major changes that have occurred in this respect since the second World War. It will be seen that the international capital market, which operated reasonably efficiently until it broke down during the series of crises of the 'thirties, was unable in Europe simply to resume in the 'fifties where it had left off a quarter of a century earlier. This was particularly so concerning London.

Chapter 5 indicates the solution resorted to by the London market in an effort to make good its own deficiencies as well as the deficiencies of continental markets, by assuming the rôle of an entrepôt for foreign capital. An attempt is made to list the special requirement that are called for in order that such a market should function satisfactorily.

The practice that has actually developed is familiar to relatively few people outside those directly concerned. It is described in some detail in Chapter 6 which deals with problems such as the types of investors interested in the bonds, the composition of issuing consortia and underwriting syndicates which handle such transactions, the discrepancies between the terms of the various issues, the types of borrowers making use of the new facilities, etc.

The 'secondary market', enabling investors and dealers to buy and sell Euro-bonds after they have been issued is described in Chapter 7.

The international structure of long-term interest rates that exists in the Euro-bond market is sought to be analysed in Chapter 8. It bears some similarity to the international structure of short-term interest rates that has developed in the Euro-dollar market and in other Euro-currency markets. An attempt is made here to cover the multitude of influences affecting the level and trend of these international interest rates, and especially to ascertain the extent to which they are affected by interest rates in the United States.

The sphere in which the impact of Euro-bond issues is particularly evident is that of the Euro-dollar market. The relationship between the two markets is extremely involved and an attempt is made to sort it out in detail in Chapter 9.

Chapter 10 examines the impact of Euro-bond issues on foreign exchanges. This impact is, if anything, even more involved than that of Euro-bond issues on Euro-dollar rates. Anyone who hopes to find a short answer to the important question of how these issues affect the dollar will see from this chapter that it all depends on how the dollars are raised for the loans and how the borrowers use the proceeds.

The following chapter deals with the impact of Euro-bond issues on domestic interest rates in the United States, in lending countries, in intermediary countries and in borrowing countries. It will be seen that those impacts are manifold and that some of them are potentially far-reaching.

While foreign loans issued in European markets in terms of U.S. dollars have been the most widely applied solution, bonds have been issued also in other denominations. Outstanding in importance are issues in terms of D. marks, covered in Chapter 12. Second in importance among non-dollar Euro-bonds are those issued in terms of a composite unit of account. That experiment, which opens up interesting possibilities, is dealt with in some detail in Chapter 13.

Chapter 14 deals with the increased extent to which the United States has come to make use of the Euro-bond market for financing direct investments abroad. The following chapter describes and examines the formula which this American borrowing in Europe mainly assumes – the issue of convertible bonds. Chapter 16 examines the basic influences that are liable to affect the trend of market prices and issue terms of straight bonds and of convertible bonds.

The next chapter is devoted to the market in investment dollars, the currency which U.K. residents would have to use if they wished to subscribe to Euro-bond issues or to acquire any other foreign securities. Even though at the time of writing the prohibitive premium on investment dollars prevents their frequent use for buying bonds, I deemed it necessary to cover the subject at some length, not so much on account of its present bearing on our main subject as owing to its potential import-ance. I took the opportunity provided by the publication of this revised edition for bringing this technical material up to date and deal with the changes brought about by the reinforce-ment of the relevant provisions of exchange control.

Some additional broader implications of the subject are

dealt with in Chapter 18. Among others, the question whether Euro-bond issues tend to increase international liquidity or whether they consolidate fluid dollar balances will be examined. An answer is sought on the question whether they have an equilibrating or a disequilibrating effect on the balance of payments and whether their effect on the internationalisation of finance is on balance an advantage or a disadvantage.

In the concluding chapter a prognosis is made about the future development of the system. The possibilities of its eclipse through various conceivable influences are examined and the probable trend of its further evolution is sought to be forecast. Very few people believed at the time when I was working on the first edition of this book that the development of the Euro-bond market constituted an institutional change that could assume permanent character. In the meantime it has become evident that, barring crises comparable with those experienced in the 'thirties, the Euro-bond market has come to stay.

Whatever the future may hold, the new device has, to date, served very useful purposes. The formula chosen by the European capital markets – to issue foreign loans in terms of dollars or some other foreign unit – has gone a long way towards assisting in the revival of foreign issuing activities outside the United States. While there is room for two opinions about the highly controversial question whether the development and expansion of the Euro-currency system is likely to be beneficial on balance it is incontestable that, during the brief period of their existence, the advantages of Euro-bonds have greatly outweighed their disadvantages.

A feature of the Euro-bond system that needs stressing from the very outset is its overwhelmingly international character both from the point of view of its issuing and marketing mechanism and from the point of view of its investing public. Its emergence has constituted an important step towards the progressive internationalisation of finance.

CHAPTER TWO

Requirements of Capital Markets

ALTHOUGH international capital movements have an extensive literature, no systematic effort seems to have been made to codify the rules defining the requirements of a good market for the issue of foreign loans. Books published on capital markets before the war or since devote most of their attention to the theory of international capital movements in their relation to the balance of payments, or they describe in detail the London capital market without displaying any special interest in foreign issuing activity. In my book *The Fight for Financial Supremacy*, published in 1931, I sought to compare the facilities of London, New York, Paris, Amsterdam and Switzerland for the issue of foreign bonds. A report published shortly before the war by the Royal Institute of International Affairs examines in some detail the conditions in which financial centres can fulfil that function satisfactorily. It is confined, however, to an examination of the three principal capital markets of the inter-war period and it was only interested in certain aspects of the subject. Nor have other books listed in our Bibliography covered the theoretical or practical problems of international bond issues in adequate detail. A book published by the *Neue Zürcher Zeitung* in 1959 covered a wide range of financial centres, and its practical material was up to date, but it was factual rather than analytical.

By far the most useful publication, from the point with which we are here concerned, is the Report of the United States Treasury, *A Description and Analysis of Certain European Capital Markets*, to which reference was made in the last chapter. It deals with some half-dozen capital markets and contains a wealth of relevant factual material, reinforced by statistical tables, which lends itself for serving as a basis of comparison between the relative merits of the various markets. It provided excellent raw material to enable us to elaborate for ourselves a set of rules on the requirements of markets for foreign issues. The first edition of this book was based extensively on that material. It is brought up to date in this edition in the light of experience during the intervening years.

It is necessary to discriminate between requirements of bond markets according to whether the new issues floated in it are for domestic or foreign borrowers, according to whether the loans which are issued for foreign borrowers are in terms of the currency of the issuing market or in some other unit, and according to whether the loans are taken up by residents or non-residents in the issuing country.

The rules applicable to capital markets whose function is confined to that of entrepôt of foreign capital will be examined in Chapter 5. The present chapter undertakes the examination of the requirements of a capital market for issues, domestic or foreign, taken up by investors in the countries in which the issue is floated. From an international financial point of view the capacity of capital markets to absorb domestic issues reduces the demand which would otherwise compete for the capital resources of foreign financial centres, in addition to competing for the capital resources of the country concerned available for lending abroad.

In many respects there is no difference between the conditions that a capital market has to fulfil in order to function satis-factorily in respect of domestic capital issues and in respect of foreign capital issues. The following are the general requirements that a good market for long-term capital issues, whether for domestic or foreign purposes, has to fulfil:

(1) It must have plentiful supplies of accumulated capital available, with an ample and continuous stream of new capital supplies to replenish its resources.

(2) There must be an investing public in the country con-cerned able and willing to absorb large amounts of new issues.

(3) It must possess financial houses that are experienced in handling capital issues and inspire confidence among investors.

(4) It must have adequate numbers of financial institutions which are able and willing to underwrite capital issues.

(5) Credit facilities must be freely available for issuing houses and underwriters that finance capital issues, pending the absorption of such issues by the investing public.

(6) Adequate information on the capital issue must be available to subscribers and investors.

(7) There must be a reasonable degree of competition between issuing houses, also between underwriters.

(8) The currency in terms of which the securities are issued must inspire a reasonable degree of confidence.

(9) Economic conditions in the country in which the issues are made must be reasonably stable.

(10) Political conditions and prospects in that country must inspire a reasonable degree of confidence.

(11) There must be an adequate number of creditworthy borrowers wanting to avail themselves of the facilities offered by market.

(12) The level of interest rates must be such as to be acceptable to borrowers of good standing.

(13) The issuing centre must possess a good Stock Exchange with a reasonably large turnover in the types of securities issues.

(14) There must be no ban on new issues.

(15) There must be no excessive official interference with new issues, for the sake of securing absolute priority for certain types of investment.

(16) There must be no excessive official borrowing that would drain the market's capital resources.

(17) Stamp duties on new issues and on transfers of securities when they change hands subsequently must not be too high.

(18) Other costs of new issues must not be excessive.

(19) Taxation on personal investment incomes and on corporation incomes must not be excessive.

(20) Monetary policy must not cause or tolerate undue instability in the market for long-term loans.

The basic condition of a capital market is the existence of adequate supplies of capital. That is the reason why countries with otherwise advanced economies do not always possess good capital markets. For instance, although Germany was between the wars one of the most highly developed countries, the wholesale destruction of her capital resources by inflation after the first World War made it impossible for her to cover her domestic capital requirements during the 'twenties. To give a more recent instance, although the industrialisation of Italy and Japan has reached an advanced stage and they have a highly developed banking system, the inadequacy of their accumulated savings has so far prevented them from developing capital markets capable of meeting their own capital requirements, let alone contributing extensively towards meeting requirements of other countries. It is of course conceivable that a capital market without adequate domestic financial resources of its own is able to borrow abroad extensively and to re-lend borrowed capital to domestic or foreign borrowers.

The Report of the United States Treasury on European capital markets provides a mass of factual and statistical material on the savings available in the capital markets of the Western European countries it covers. Each chapter dealing with individual countries examines closely the amounts of such savings by individuals, business firms and Government departments. The capital available for new issues may assume the form of liquid assets accumulated by the private sector of the economy – individual investors, business firms, insurance companies, investment trusts and unit trusts, family trusts, charitable trusts, pension funds, etc. – or they may be owned by the public sector – reserves of pension and national insurance funds, assets of savings banks, funds handled by the Public Trustee, etc.

Even the most plentiful supplies of accumulated savings are

not inexhaustible. Growing economies and steadily rising prices mean ever-increasing capital requirements, and they can only be met out of a steadily increasing stream of new savings, both personal and institutional. No capital market can expand if it merely turns over on past savings, because the rate of replacement of its capital resources is kept down unduly by over-consumption or by high taxation.

In itself the mere existence of liquid resources available for investment in new issues would not be sufficient to ensure their success, unless those owning or controlling the resources are actively interested in the type of investment these issues represent. If those with whom the decision rests are not accustomed to invest in long-term securities, or if they are prevented by legal or conventional inhibitions from acquiring such securities, or if for some reasons they have no confidence in them, no capital market can develop. This is one of the main reasons why the capacity of the French market to absorb bond issues bears no relation to the high stage of development attained by the financial system of France, or to the volume of her financial resources.

In some countries savings assume mainly the form of hoarded gold or notes, or savers may prefer to retain their liquidity by keeping their savings in the form of bank deposits or savings bank deposits. Banks which hold their savings may not be in the habit of investing in long-term securities outside the Gilt-edged market. Disastrous experience such as the German inflation, or the French currency depreciation, or wholesale defaults by borrowers, is liable to discourage individual investors from acquiring long-term securities. In such situations capital markets depend largely on institutional investors and public investors. In any case, all modern capital markets have in fact come to depend to a large and increasing extent on such investors rather than on the multitude of individual investors, though the latter still play a sufficiently important part to influence the capacity of the capital market to absorb systematically large and frequent capital issues.

In addition to the employment of new savings in new issues,

the capital market provides facilities for turning over existing investments. This is usually practiced on a fairly large scale. But markets for new issues cannot depend for their sole or main source of capital on the investors' willingness to switch their investments. In any case the process entails a depreciation of existing securities, sold out for the sake of being able to reinvest the proceeds, and if this occurs systematically over a period it is liable to discourage demand for new issues. At any rate, it raises their interest rates, influenced by yields on existing securities. Capital gains tax also discourages investment switchings.

The possession of large capital resources and the willingness of their owners to invest in long-term securities would be of limited use if the market did not also possess efficient institutions capable of collecting these resources from willing investors and passing them on to those who want to borrow them. The actual mechanism that fulfils this function varies from country to country.

Under the American system the banking group that handles the issue includes a very large number of financial houses each of which takes over an agreed proportion of the amount available and is directly responsible for placing its share with investors. Bondsellers who pay visits to potential buyers play an important part in the placing of new issues, and a very high proportion of the bonds find their way to the public through sales over the counter of the issuing banks.

Under the traditional British system two sets, and possibly three sets, of financial houses are engaged in the operation. The issues are floated by one single issuing house, or a very small number of issuing houses. There is, in addition, a syndicate of underwriters who are not required to handle the issue in the first instance, and may not be called upon to handle it at all even at a later stage, but merely assume between them the risk that the issue may not be covered in full by applications of subscribers. If the loan is covered their function ceases. It is only if the loan is not covered fully that underwriters have to take over their percentage of the amount left uncovered, and they then become responsible for placing it with investors. There may be a third set of institutions, the sub-underwriters who relieve underwriters of part of the risk that the latter had assumed. Members of this group are usually large investors who are prepared to keep the securities as part of their port-folios, or stockbrokers who can depend on receiving a number of applications for the issue from their regular customer.

In France new issues are placed to a large degree by means of sales over the counter by banks. For this reason the participa-tion in every issuing group of a commercial bank possessing many branches is considered essential to ensure the success of the operation.

What really matters is that there should be a sufficiently large number of financially strong firms able and willing to carry loans which cannot be placed with investors immediately, and to wait until the market has settled down sufficiently to enable them to unload gradually their holdings without forcing down the price. The number of participating firms and their total resources available for that purpose must be sufficiently large to enable them to absorb and carry fairly substantial amounts of such 'undigested' issues, so that the market does not become hope-lessly congested as a result of partial failures of a few issues.

Public issues are highly involved operations calling for a great deal of technical knowledge of accountancy, law, publicity, Stock Exchange technique, etc. In order to be able to judge the debtor's capacity to pay, issuing houses must be qualified to assess his financial position and prospects, also the economic background on which his position is conditioned in the long run. They must also be well informed about political conditions and prospects in the borrower's country and in the world at large.

It is also essential that the banking houses engaged in such operations should enjoy high prestige and should inspire con-fidence among the investing public. Their name should be of such a high standing that its presence on the prospectus should in itself go a long way towards ensuring the success of the operation. To that end it is important that the past record of issuing houses should be good. It is true, issuing houses have no legal responsibility for the losses suffered by investors through defaults by debtors on bonds issued by them. Nevertheless, it is to their interest to select with great care the transactions they handle and to avoid as far as possible risking such defaults, each of which is likely to be remembered against them on future occasions, unless the defaults were due to some unpredictable *force majeure* over which the debtors had no control, such as a world war. It is to the interest of issuing houses to scrutinise the proposed transactions with the utmost care and to satisfy themselves as far as this is humanly possible that the debtors are likely to be both willing and able to meet their engagements.

Houses of good standing are indeed short-sighted if they handle loans for debtors with a bad record or with unpromising prospects. They might earn an immediate profit on such transactions, but this is liable to be paid for dearly in the long run by a deterioration of the goodwill represented by the confidence the investing public have in their judgement. Should, contrary to their expectations, a formerly reliable borrower default, houses of first-rate standing always deem it to be their foremost duty to investors as well as in accordance with their own interests to bring the utmost pressure to bear on the defaulters to induce them to meet their liabilities. Failing that, they must use their influence in their own centres and in foreign centres to ensure that the defaulters should be blacklisted until they have come to an arrangement with their existing creditors.

It is essential that a good capital market should possess adequate short-term credit facilities at reasonably low interest rates, enabling issuing houses and underwriters to carry temporarily amounts of loans not taken up by the public. The British system under which the functions of issuing houses are separated from those of commercial banks enables the former and their underwriting syndicates to draw temporarily upon the credit resources of the latter. The development of the Euro-dollar system under which banks and other institutions of good standing are able to borrow large amounts at short notice has greatly assisted the capital markets in respect of securing funds for the provisional financing of bond issues.

Investors may be reluctant to risk their capital by subscribing to new issues unless they can depend on being able to obtain subsequently reliable and prompt information relevant to the position and prospects of their investment. In itself the publication of the flood of information contained in prospectuses of new issues and the publicity campaign that accompanies them is not sufficient. In the long run it is to the interest of the development and maintenance of good market for new issues that there should be a reliable, well-informed and independent financial Press that is capable of keeping investors up to date with the latest developments liable to affect their investments, and that is prepared to comment on them fearlessly. Not unnaturally banks are inclined to prefer a subservient financial Press which confines itself to publication of items released or approved by them. Taking a long view, however, they are likely to find it easier to float new issues if the investing public can also depend on obtaining reliable information independently of officially-inspired material, both at the time of the new issues and subsequently.

The Report of the United States Treasury stresses the need for competition between issuing houses as one of the major conditions of a good capital market. This attitude appears to indicate that the Report was compiled by experts belonging essentially to the post-war generation. Anyone who remembers the excesses of competition for foreign loans by issuing houses during the 'twenties is bound to realise that competition need not necessarily be an unqualified blessing. Beyond doubt a quasi-monopolistic position occupied by issuing houses provides temptation and opportunity for misusing it. But there is another side to it. During the years that preceded the Wall Street slump there was an overdose of competition between relatively inexperienced New York issuing houses. As a result many would-be borrowers in Central Europe and elsewhere were inundated with competitive offers and were enabled to borrow excessive amounts on terms which had failed to allow for the extent of the risk involved. Nor was the rule that defaulters must not be allowed to borrow unless they have come to terms with their creditors observed too strictly by the over-eager would-be lenders.

Absence of competition need not necessarily be disadvantageous from the point of view of a good capital market. Under a long-established tradition of the London banking community, issuing houses specialised in certain countries before the war, and never, or hardly ever, poached on each other's preserves. This did not mean that they were in a monopolistic position, for rival offers to borrowers by American and Continental issuing houses kept their terms reasonably competitive in spite of the almost complete absence of competition within the City of London itself.

Nor is the existence of permanent underwriting arrangements by which underwriting syndicates consist of permanent members participating in new issues any disadvantage. So long as such arrangements are not misused their advantages of a steady system heavily outweigh their disadvantages.

One of the reasons why investors are apt to distrust issues with fixed interest rates is distrust in the stability of the currency of the loan contract. Apart altogether from periodically recurrent acute devaluation scares, creeping inflation tends to discourage investors from holding fixed interest-bearing securities, because it gradually reduces the purchasing power of the currency in which they are to receive interest and capital repayment. This distrust finds expression in the terms which are acceptable to subscribers. Once investors become really inflation-conscious, they might require such a high yield that borrowers of standing might be unwilling to concede them. Distrust of investors in the stability of the currency can be allayed by the issue of bonds convertible into equities, which could serve as a hedge against inflation.

Economic instability in the lending country is apt to react unfavourably on its capital market, inasmuch as it inspires distrust among investors. Unsound Budgetary policies in lending countries, apart altogether from their inflationary effect,

B

tend to discourage investors from acquiring bonds, because of anticipation of heavy Government borrowing that is liable to raise long-term interest rates in general.

Domestic or international political uncertainty, or fears of the advent of a régime hostile to investors, tend to operate in the same sense. That is one of the reasons why, within their quantitative limitations, the Swiss and Dutch capital markets compare favourably in many ways with other capital markets.

Uncertainties, whether political, financial or economic, that are liable to affect the borrowers' ability or willingness to meet their liabilities constitute one of the major obstacles to the development of active markets in foreign issues. During the 'thirties and again during the early post-war years, very few foreign borrowers were looked upon as being sufficiently credit-worthy to inspire confidence among issuing houses, under-writers and investors. Even in the 'sixties the number of those who pass muster was relatively small, though it was sufficient to ensure an active issue market.

Reference was made above to the possibility of circumstances in which potential borrowers of high standing are unwilling to pay sufficiently high interest rates to induce investors to sub-scribe. Considerations of prestige deter first-rate borrowers from paying interest rates which had been charged to second-rate borrowers in the past. Interest rates are liable to become prohibitive through measures to defend the exchange. If general demand for capital exceeds supply considerably interest rates are liable to rise to a level at which demand by good-class borrowers becomes automatically discouraged. During periods of inflation, however, many industrial borrowers who stand to benefit by the rising trend of prices are apt to disregard high interest rates, owing to their ability to pass on the additional cost they represent. Rising or high interest rates are not, there-fore, an absolute obstacle to the maintenance of an active new issue market.

In order to ensure a steady interest of investors in new issues they must have the assurance that they are able to realise their securities easily and at competitive prices whenever they feel inclined to do so. That end is assured if the securities are listed on a good Stock Exchange. The larger is the turnover the lower is the cost of transferring stocks to other investors, because in a wide market it is easy to find a counterpart for a large buying or selling order without moving the price unduly against the buyer or the seller who takes the initiative. But the Euro-bond market has achieved a large turnover outside Stock Exchanges.

Freedom from official restrictions, statutory or otherwise, on new issues is an important condition. But the need to apply for licence to authorise individual issues need not in itself unduly handicap a capital market, provided that the authorities are reasonably liberal in granting such licenses. Nor is official co-ordination of public issues in order to avoid a rush by borrowers that would cause a congestion of the market, by itself an obstacle.

Over-spending by the Government or by local authorities is liable to be detrimental to the development of a good capital market for private borrowers, not only because it tends to raise interest rates but also because the priority that official borrowing is apt to be given, officially or otherwise, tends to drain the market of resources available for other purposes.

If the authorities lay down a too rigid list of priorities among non-official borrowers it may effectively prevent access to the market by borrowers with a low priority. Even a *de facto* priority, such as enjoyed by the financing of mortgages in Germany, is apt to handicap the development of a good capital market for other borrowers.

Unduly high stamp duties on new issues, by raising the cost of such transactions, tend to discourage them. If the demand is sufficiently strong, however, borrowers are willing to pay this once-for-all expense, unless they are able to find alternative markets where the cost of new issues is lower, or unless they find alternative ways of covering their capital requirements. The attitude of investors is liable to be influenced also by the high cost of subsequent transfers of securities. They expect borrowers to make the terms of the issues sufficiently attractive to compensate them for that cost, although if the duty is payable by the buyer and not by the seller of the securities its effect on the attitude of subscribers to new issues may not be too pronounced. In the case of bearer bonds transfer tax does not arise, but in some countries a once-for-all levy is payable when they are issued.

Costs other than stamp duties connected with new issues – publicity expenses, legal expenses, accountants' fees, etc. – are liable to affect the efficiency of new issue markets. A widening of the spread between the net proceeds received by borrowers and the amounts lent by investors may discourage both parties. Lenders are certain to insist on terms which secure for them the net yield they feel they are entitled to receive to make the investment worth their while.

A high general level of taxation on investment incomes is also apt to discourage activity in capital markets. If their taxed income from the investment is too low they may feel it is not worth their while to take the risk involved in investing for the sake of such inadequate return. For this reason capital markets in a country with a relatively low level of taxation on investment incomes are at an advantage over the capital market of a country with a higher level of taxation. The latter is likely to confine its lendings to highly creditworthy borrowers, as their taxed yield on even moderately speculative bonds would not compensate them adequately for the risk involved, especially if capital gains are taxed heavily.

Last but by no means least, it is an essential condition if a good capital market that the prices of bonds should not fluctuate unduly as a result of monetary policy measures. Speculative risk resulting from violent ups and downs of securities caused by such measures is liable to discourage demand for new issues, unless their terms are sufficiently favourable to investors to compensate them for such risk. Under the conception that prevailed until quite recently it was considered to be outside the scope of monetary policy, as distinct from debt management policy, to interfere with the trend of bond prices. According to the new conception developed under the influence of the

Radcliffe Report and the American Report on Money and Credit, monetary policy has to aim, however, at influencing the entire structure of interest rates instead of confining itself to influencing short-term interest rates only. This new policy is still in its infancy, but it seems conceivable that its development might affect the facilities of capital markets unfavourably if unexpected changes in monetary policy should exaggerate the effects of changes in short-term interest rates on the trend of bond prices.

All the above requirements apply to markets for domestic as well as foreign issues. There are, however, a number of additional requirements which are peculiar to markets for the issue of foreign securities:

(1) The country of the issuing market must have a basically favourable trend in its balance of payments.

(2) The currency of that country must not be regarded by borrowers as one involving the risk of a revaluation.

(3) It must not be regarded by investors as involving a risk of devaluation.

(4) Domestic requirements enjoying *de jure* or *de facto* priority must not absorb an unduly large proportion of the capital resources available.

(5) There must be no ban on foreign issues or even an unduly restrictive licensing system.

(6) The currency of the lending country must not be subject to exchange restrictions of the kind that would prevent or gravely handicap the issue of foreign securities or subsequent dealings in them.

(7) It is an advantage if the issuing centre has a good foreign exchange market.

(8) It is an advantage if the issuing centre has good facilities for the short-term investment of the proceeds of foreign loans by borrowers.

The efficiency of a capital market, even for purely domestic issues, is liable to be affected by the state of the balance of payments. It is liable to affect decisively the ability and willingness of lending countries to lend abroad. Taking a long view, it is essential for such countries to have a reasonably steady export surplus which, unless lent abroad in the form of long-term loans, would assume the form of additional short-term claims or would lead to an increase of the gold reserve.

Although this may now appear beyond controversy, not so very long ago the opposite view – that a country which lends abroad in excess of its export surplus is in a position automatically to increase its export surplus as a result of such overlending – was firmly held by many economists in Britain. It was a quasi-religious belief, based on Britain's favourable experience during the 19th century when her balance of payments position was so strong that she could safely overlend on the firm assumption that sooner or later the amount overlent would come to be spent on British goods or services. The unofficial embargo on foreign loans imposed during the 'twenties had been strongly opposed on the basis of pre-1914 experience, in total disregard of the change in Britain's fundamental situation. The reason why Britain had been safe in overlending before 1914 was that her goods had been competitive. After 1918 she was no longer safe in overlending because, with sterling overvalued, her goods were no longer sufficiently competitive, and because meanwhile structural changes developed to her detriment. In the changed circumstances overlending tended to result in a decline of her gold reserve and/or an accumulation of her foreign short-term indebtedness.

Amidst conditions prevailing between the wars, and in more recent times, Britain ought to have cut her coat according to her cloth, instead of assuming that the cloth would be forthcoming in the required length regardless of the way in which her coat was cut. She could only afford to export capital to the extent of the surplus of her balance of payments. Disregard of the rule carried its penalty in the form of pressure on sterling, loss of gold which she could ill afford to lose, and increase of foreign short-term liabilities.

In practice the rule need not apply rigidly to every single year. If a country has a large gold reserve or if it is in a position to attract short-term balances easily it is able to grant long-term loans abroad over a number of years even if it has no correspondingly favourable trade balance available for that purpose. This is what happened in the United States during the late 'fifties and early 'sixties. Year after year the New York market handled large foreign issues, even though the balance of payments was persistently unfavourable. Unlike Britain during the 'twenties, however, the United States in the 'fifties was in a strong enough position to be able to afford a decline in her gold reserve and an increase in her short-term liabilities resulting from long-term overlending.

A capital market for foreign loans is not satisfactory unless the country concerned is able to meet temporary ups and downs of its balance of payments, as distinct from a perennial deficit, without having to resort to measures leading on each occasion to a drastic curtailment of foreign long-term borrowing.

While from the lenders' point of view it is essential that the currency of the transaction does not involve a devaluation risk, from the borrower's point of view it is equally important that it does not involve a revaluation risk. First-rate borrowers who are in a position to say 'no' would only be prepared to borrow in a currency which is liable to appreciate if they could do so on very favourable terms. Likewise, if the currency of the loan contract is liable to depreciate investors are reluctant to hold such loans unless their yield is sufficiently high to make it appear worth their while to take the risk.

From time to time most currencies are bound to be suspected of involving either the risk of devaluation or the risk of revaluation. The situation and prospects of a currency are liable to change with disconcerting suddenness, and seldom is a currency entirely above suspicion from the point of view of both potential borrowers and potential lenders for any length of time. But in the prolonged absence of acute devaluation scares or revaluation scares certain currencies may become reasonably acceptable to both parties.

From the point of view of foreign issuing activity it is essential that there should be enough capital resources for domestic as well as foreign requirements. Otherwise, even in the absence of official priorities in favour of domestic borrowers, pressure of domestic demand might raise long-term interest rates to a level at which it ceases to be attractive to foreign borrowers. In some countries, moreover, domestic requirements of certain categories have an admitted prior claim for capital resources, in which case the possibility of developing a foreign loan market depends on the existence of surplus resources in excess of those earmarked for domestic requirements.

The absence of exchange restrictions of a kind that would prevent their issue is an essential requirement of a market for foreign loans. Under controlled exchange the granting of permits to issue foreign loans may be determined not only by priorities of domestic capital requirements but also by requirements of foreign exchange situation.

It is an advantage if the lending country has a good foreign exchange market which would enable the debtor to withdraw the proceeds of a loan as and when required, to sell forward those portions of the loan which are to be transferred later, and to cover the amounts required subsequently for interest payments and capital repayments in a way that is the most convenient. This is not indispensable, however, so long as there are no exchange restrictions to prevent the borrower from selling the proceeds of the loan in some other market, or from surrendering them to the monetary authorities of his own country. The existence of good money market facilities that enable borrowers to employ temporarily the proceeds of the loan pending their transfer is also an advantage.

Such temporary investment of the loan proceeds need not be effected in the local currency of the lending country. Thanks to the development of the Euro-currency markets, borrowers are in a position to employ the proceeds, pending their use for the purpose for which they were borrowed, in Euro-dollars or in other Euro-currency deposits.

Foreign issuing activity is stimulated by the existence of a buyers' market in the goods exported by the lending country. If such goods have a sellers' market the exporting country need not go out of its way to increase its exports by granting long-term loans to the importers. But difficulties in finding markets abroad, and keen foreign competition, tend to induce industries and their Governments to provide loan facilities as an inducement for importers to buy their goods.

CHAPTER THREE

Pre-War Markets in Foreign Issues

This chapter deals with describing the extent to which the requirements of a good capital market for foreign issues, as enumerated in the last chapter, had existed before the first World War and during the inter-war period. It is always tempting to look back upon past periods with nostalgia and to regard them as pictures of perfection by comparison with the less satisfactory state of affairs prevailing in more recent times. Our difficulties of yesterday never appear to be as difficult as our difficulties of today. But even allowing for this, there can be no doubt that in this instance our nostalgia is justified. The international capital markets of the 19th century and of the early 20th century had their shortcomings and had been subject to much criticism in contemporary financial literature. Nevertheless, in this case the picture of near-perfection which we conjure up when glancing back on those days is substantially correct, at any rate in a relative sense. The leading capital markets of the day – London, Paris and Berlin, and later New York – had conformed to ideal requirements to a degree which in our days may well appear to us to be bordering on the unattainable.

To what extent did European capital markets conform to the requirements of a good market enumerated in the last chapter before the first World War? London and other capital markets had, generally speaking, plentiful supplies of funds available for investment. In the prolonged absence of major wars and amidst conditions of economic and political stability prevailing most of the time, savings were accumulating very satisfactorily. Throughout the 19th century and up to the first World War saving was generally looked upon as one of the major civic virtues. Keynes's immortal remark that 'after all, even a rich man may enter the Kingdom of Heaven if only he saved', truly expressed the prevailing attitude. There was not only willingness but also ample opportunity for saving. Distribution of wealth and income was unequal to a high degree – and, in accordance with the elementary principles of Keynesian economics, this meant that a high proportion of it could be saved. Nor did Governments mop up for their own requirements the funds available through saving. Generally speaking, budgets were balanced, at any rate in the leading countries possessing capital markets. In Britain the public debt was £656 million in 1914 compared with its peak figure of £848 million reached as a result of the Napoleonic Wars – an actual reduction by nearly £200 million between the end of those wars and the beginning of the first World War. Accumulated savings were left at the disposal of private enterprise at home and abroad, and of foreign Governments in need of loans.

There was in each of the principal lending centres, and also in smaller countries such as Holland, Switzerland, Belgium and Sweden, an investing public accustomed to subscribe to foreign bond issues and it was encouraged to do so by the stable monetary conditions prevailing between the battle of Waterloo and the first battle of the Marne. During earlier centuries borrowers had depended mainly on loans from powerful banking firms, but by the second half of the 19th century and even more the early part of the 20th century the broader investing public came to be able and willing to participate extensively in such transactions and to supply the bulk of the capital required. Their combined resources exceeded considerably any conceivable amounts that even the richest banking houses, or any combination of them, would have been able to lend.

The capital markets were well served by banks experienced in the art of issuing securities. In addition to old-established merchant banking firms, the more recently created commercial banks in continental centres – though not in London – came to lend a hand to ensure the success of the operation. The system of underwriting new issues, though not altogether unknown in earlier centuries, developed during the 19th century and reached a very advanced stage, making for a higher degree of stability in the capital markets. Before the existence of underwriting syndicates in the modern sense, terms of bond issues had to be fixed in such a way as to allow a very wide safety margin so as to ensure that the public took up the entire amount. During the 18th century several British lottery loans were issued by the Government on such generous terms that they opened with premiums of up to 12 per cent. By the close of the 19th century it became possible to cut margins much finer, thanks largely to the development of the system of underwriting.

The development of modern money markets, especially in London, provided great assistance to the market for capital issues. Issuing houses and underwriters were able to raise short-term funds to tide them over any temporary difficulties in placing the loans with the public.

A financial Press which was virtually non-existent in earlier centuries developed in the principal capital markets during the early 19th century. Although there was no lack of outspoken comment, the general attitude of financial commentators during the period preceding the first World War had not adequately conformed to the requirements of a well-informed financial Press, independent and fearless in its new service and in its comments. Indeed, right up to the early inter-war period the financial Press in general was much too timid and subservient when dealing with banks of importance. However, during the 'twenties and 'thirties gradually a more independent spirit came to prevail.

Before the first World War there was adequate, and at times more than adequate, competition between rival financial houses engaged in loan operations. Nevertheless, from time to time in certain sections of the market a leading bank or a group of banks succeeded in achieving a quasi-monopolistic position.

By and large, borrowers had succeeded in securing for themselves the terms that they deserved through their past record as debtors, their position at the time of the issue and their prospects. Between the wars, during the 'twenties, the pendulum swung in the opposite direction, in that cut-throat competition developed between rival financial centres as well as between rival firms in the same centres – though London issuing houses had upheld their tradition of abstaining from poaching on each other's preserves. Excessive competition among issuing houses caused unwarranted reductions of long-term interest rates on loans to borrowers with dubious prospects. As I pointed out in the last chapter, borrowers in Central Europe in particular were allowed to raise capital in amounts and on terms which had failed to allow for the extent of the risk involved.

Investors had absolute confidence in the stability of currencies in which loans were issued before the first World War. Fluctuations of those currencies were negligible and there was no such thing as exchange control. Devaluation scares and revaluation scares, too, were non-existent. The currency chaos resulting from the first World War came to an end during the 'twenties, and after the restoration of monetary stability the investing public came to trust the principal currencies once more. Although the dollar was easily the hardest amongst them, and the French franc after its stabilisation became harder than sterling during the late 'twenties, there was no difficulty whatsoever for London issuing houses to issue foreign loans in terms of sterling.

Before the first World War the process of long-term lending conformed to a high degree to the requirements of general economic stability. Broadly speaking, surplus countries were willing to lend to deficit countries the surpluses available for that purpose, and highly developed countries were lending to developing countries. Things were not nearly so satisfactory between the wars. By that time Germany became a heavy borrower of capital in order to replace the capital wiped out by inflation. Until the late 'twenties France had more than enough domestic economic troubles and these, together with the heavy losses inflicted on French investors by defaults and repudiations of foreign loans, left them reluctant to resume lending abroad. Britain had to struggle with chronic unemployment resulting from the overvaluation of sterling and from structural economic changes. She was overlending from time to time and had to re-borrow abroad the resulting deficit on capital account. The largest lender, the United States, was in the throes of an unprecedented domestic boom which was fated to come to a bad end, even though few people realised it until October 1929. So long as it lasted it attracted foreign capital to New York, which meant that capital was flowing 'uphill' – from deficit countries to a surplus country. The absence of ideal equilibrium did not however, prevent the lending countries from operating successfully and on an extensive scale.

Before the first World War *pax Britannica* ensured the necessary degree of international political stability for the satisfactory working of international capital markets. During the first half of the inter-war period, too, the international political outlook was satisfactory, as another major war was considered most unlikely. By the time the prospects became troubled by the advent of the Nazi régime, capital issuing activity came to a standstill in any case everywhere, as a result of the crises and the prolonged depression in the 'thirties.

There was no lack of creditworthy borrowers before the first World War. Although defaults by debtors were not infrequent, many countries honoured their financial undertakings very scrupulously and were always welcome whenever they wanted to raise more capital. All loans did not serve constructive purposes, however. France in particular was inclined to lend too much to her political allies to assist in financing their military preparations. As a result of the revolution in Russia and of political and financial difficulties in Eastern Europe, a very high proportion of pre-1914 loans came to be defaulted upon. Nevertheless, by the middle 'twenties lending centres were once more willing to lend and there were more than enough borrowers that were looked upon as creditworthy. Many of the defaulting debtors came to terms with their creditors and were able to resume borrowing abroad.

The level of long-term interest rates before 1914 was low. Although it rose considerably as a result of the first World War, it gradually declined during the 'twenties. Differentials in interest charges to various borrowers did not always express reasonably their relative creditworthiness, but broadly speaking all good borrowers were able to raise capital on tolerable terms. There were ample Stock Exchange facilities in the principal financial markets and also in the smaller centres for dealing in bonds subsequent to their issue.

Bans on issues were unknown before 1914, but Britain felt impelled to introduce between the wars a system of unofficial co-ordination of new issues which became formalised later with the establishment of the Capital Issues Committee.

Before the first World War there was very little official borrowing in the capital market by the authorities in the lending countries, except for the purpose of re-financing. Between the wars, too, until the Wall Street slump most of the market's capital resources were available for private requirements. During the long depression there was considerable Government borrowing for the purpose of financing public works to create employment, especially in the United States, and in the late 'thirties there was much new borrowing for rearmament. But during the 'thirties private demand for capital by eligible borrowers was in any case at a low ebb.

Taxes on new issues and transfers were very low everywhere until the post-war period. They certainly did not discourage issuing activities. Before 1914 direct taxation on interest income was very low. It rose considerably after the first World War, but even then it had not reached a level that would have discouraged issuing activities.

Throughout the 19th century and even more during the inter-war period monetary policy measures that had to be adopted for various reasons did handicap capital issuing activity from time to time, especially in London where the Bank of England pursued the traditions of widely fluctuating Bank rate. The Paris capital market was at an advantage because Bank rate changes were infrequent. In London whenever the Bank rate was raised to a high level, capital issuing activity in general and the issue of foreign loans in particular were temporarily discouraged. By and large, however, neither this nor the Stock Exchange fluctuations caused by the British monetary policy measures acted as a deterrent to capital issuing activities.

The extent to which the special requirements of a good market for foreign loans prevailed declined considerably before the second World War. As already observed earlier in this chapter, the lending countries had by and large favourable balances of payments before 1914. Apart from a few isolated bad years, Britain had a substantial perennial export surplus – allowing of course for invisible exports – and so had France and Germany. Britain's surplus declined after the first World War, while the French surplus on current account was more than wiped out by the flight of French capital. After the stabilisation of the franc at an undervalued level, the current export surplus was reinforced by repatriation of French capital, and ample resources became available for lending abroad. But owing to the heavy losses suffered by French investors on their pre-1914 foreign bonds, foreign issuing activity in Paris was well below the surplus available for that purpose. As for the United States her export surpluses during the inter-war period were inclined to be embarrassingly large. In addition there was a flow of capital to Wall Street during the 'twenties. American foreign lending was indeed on a large scale throughout the 'twenties, but a large part of it was thus re-borrowed.

Until the series of crises initiated by the Wall Street slump lenders and borrowers had no cause to fear revaluation or devaluation of the currencies in terms of which the foreign loans were issued. Loans in terms of sterling, dollars or other hard currencies were equally acceptable to all parties. Nevertheless, American issuing houses sought to safeguard the investors' interests by inserting a gold clause in the loan contracts. That clause was declared invalid by an Act passed in 1933.

There were no priorities for domestic borrowing which would have interfered with foreign issuing activities. We already saw that after the return to the gold standard Britain introduced, however, an unofficial embargo on foreign loans. During the 'thirties that embargo came to be reinforced and regularised, and was eventually made statutory. In practice foreign borrowers actually enjoyed priority in the London market before the second World War, because most issuing houses confined their activities to foreign loans and barely touched domestic capital issues.

Exchange restrictions were unknown during the years before 1914 and even during the inter-war period they barely affected the lending centres. On the other hand, restrictions operating in potential borrowing countries in the 'thirties tended to discourage long-term lending. All lending centres had good foreign exchange markets for the requirements of borrowers. There were also excellent short-term investment facilities in London and New York, in which borrowers were able to employ temporarily the unspent parts of their loans.

Although conditions in capital markets for the issue of foreign loans were not so favourable during the inter-war period as they had been before 1914, they were on the whole adequate and, until the advent of the crisis of the 'thirties, quite satisfactory. That crisis inflicted heavy losses on creditors, many of whom had already suffered losses in consequence of the first World War and its aftermaths. The need for defending the currencies of lending countries, the advent of exchange control, and economic nationalism during the 'thirties between them drastically curtailed capital issuing activity. Such were the changes for the worse that it was indeed surprising that some of that activity revived at all in the late 'thirties, even if it was a bare fraction of the volume it had attained before 1914 and during the foreign issue boom of the 'twenties. The crisis of the 'thirties led to a widespread abandonment of the liberal policies towards foreign lending that had developed during the stable conditions of the 19th century. The outbreak of the second World War brought issuing activity for private purposes virtually to a standstill. Foreign lending came to assume the form of inter-Government transactions.

CHAPTER FOUR

Post-War Markets in Foreign Issues

INTERNATIONAL capital markets were very slow in recovering from the effects of the crises of the 'thirties and of their virtually complete suspension during the second World War. For a long time during the post-war period general conditions did not favour a resumption of their activities, even though two of the markets, New York and Zurich, emerged from the war more or less unimpaired. In London, large foreign sterling balances, exchange controls, currency uncertainties and political uncertainties resulting from the cold war tended to discourage for a long time a resumption of foreign issues. But in any case, a resumption of foreign issues would have received scant encouragement under the Labour Government, even if conditions had been favourable to it. The Chancellor of the Exchequer, Dr. Dalton, was openly hostile to international financial activities on ideological grounds. His attitude and that of his Government was characterised by a reply when pressed in Parliament to do something about the suspension of payments on the Japanese debt to British investors, to the effect that it served the British bondholders right if they lost their money – why did they lend to Japan?

Capital resources available for foreign loans were curtailed during the post-war period partly by the effect of creeping inflation and partly by post-war equalitarianism as a result of which a smaller proportion of incomes tended to be saved. Moreover, in accordance with the spirit of the times, a larger proportion of corporation earnings was ploughed back into the firms instead of being made available to shareholders for reinvestment. On the other hand, capital requirements of the public sector of the economy greatly increased as a result of large Budgetary deficits through increased public spending on capital projects and the requirements of nationalised industries. There were, moreover, abnormal domestic capital requirements of the private sector arising from physical reconstruction of war damage, re-equipment of plant worn out during the war, replenishment of greatly depleted supplies of every kind and the expansionary post-war economic policy in general.

Investors' willingness to acquire and hold fixed interest bearing securities in general and foreign bonds in particular was affected unfavourably by creeping inflation. It is true, the volume of outstanding foreign long-term indebtedness which was grossly excessive before the war declined in the meantime to more normal proportions, partly through gradual repayments in the absence of new borrowings and partly through a fall in the value of the currencies of the loan contracts. The same amount of foreign debt represented only about one-third of its pre-war burden in real terms, so that there was ample scope for a re-expansion of its total. Nevertheless, because past losses on foreign bonds were still remembered, owing to the post-war liquidity-preference of investors, and, above all, owing to the perennial inflationary trend, it became necessary to offer them high yields, apart from other reasons, in order to compensate them for the erosion of the purchasing power of their investment. The tendency in capital markets was distinctly in favour of equities and the yield on good-class equities declined well below that of Government loans.

London finance houses came to take an increased interest in domestic industrial capital issues. They all but lost interest in foreign loans for lack of opportunity. The same trend prevailed, though to a less pronounced extent, during the early post-war years in New York and other capital markets. However, as soon as opportunity for making foreign issues reappeared, issuing houses were able to resume where they left off some thirty years earlier. Generally speaking, issuing houses throughout the world have become in the meantime even more confidence-inspiring than they had been before the war, having weathered the banking crises of the 'thirties and having in many instances strengthened their position through amalgamations. Moreover, they increased their capital resources through becoming limited companies and attracting funds from the public instead of relying entirely on the family fortunes of their owners. Underwriting facilities have also improved because there are now many more institutional investors qualified to participate. The improvement of the machinery for foreign issues varied from country to country according to the degree of expansion of insurance companies, investment trusts, etc., and the degree of their freedom and willingness to invest in foreign loans.

Cut-throat competition that characterised the market for foreign issues during the 'twenties is no longer in evidence, but there is a sufficient degree of healthy competition to ensure fair terms for borrowers and to prevent an undue widening of the margin between what they pay and what the investors receive. Those margins vary widely according to capital market, largely owing to the differences in taxes.

Amidst the conditions of easy money that prevailed most of the time in lending countries in the early post-war years, credits for temporary financing of foreign loan operations were most of the time easily obtainable. In more recent years the development of the Euro-currency markets has added considerably to such facilities in European capital markets, and so has the creation of the inter-bank money market in London. But chronic conditions of dear money in London and some other markets during the 'sixties have added to the cost of temporary financing of foreign bond issues.

In respect of the outlook for currencies of the loan contracts the situation is incomparably less satisfactory than it had been before 1914, indeed even less satisfactory than during the 'twenties. From time to time investors came to suspect the currencies of the loan contracts of a possible devaluation, or they come to be suspected by borrowers of a possible revaluation. The pre-war formula for protection against both through the insertion of a gold clause in the loan contract – which in any case had been applied almost exclusively to dollar loans – came to be discredited through the repudiation of the gold clause by the United States. In many countries the insertion of such a clause has been made unlawful.

While before the war economic instability through deflation was the danger, during the post-war period it was replaced by uncertainty caused by economic instability through inflation. From time to time measures against inflation in lending countries came to handicap issuing activities. All the time many potential borrowers were under a cloud, owing to the acceleration of the pace of their domestic inflation. Political uncertainties, too, were much more in evidence than during the 'twenties. It is true that at the time of writing (at the beginning of 1969), acute fears of a third World War appear to have receded into the background, though there are war scares from time to time. On the other hand, the possibility of the advent of Left-wing régimes in borrowing countries is now much more perturbing to investors. There is also the practice of restrictions on lending abroad by Governments of the lending countries.

Largely as a result of creeping inflation and periodically recurrent currency scares, long-term interest rates in the London capital market have been rather high. In Paris there is a virtually complete ban on investment in foreign securities, and in any case, owing to the conditions created by the troubles in 1968, the question does not arise at the time of writing. In Germany, in spite of the existence of ample capital resources, a very large proportion of the available resources is mopped up by mortgage loans to finance building activity. Interest rates in Amsterdam and Zurich have been relatively low, but there have been official limitations on foreign issues in both countries. Since 1964 the United States adopted various devices to restrict lending abroad. These measures were reinforced in 1969.

Stock Exchange facilities are reasonably adequate in all post-war capital markets. In any case, most transactions in Euro-bonds are now done outside Stock Exchanges. Their new market is described in Chapter 7.

There are now controls of various kinds over issuing activity in most capital markets. Almost everywhere very elaborate steps have to be taken to obtain permission for foreign capital issues. In most markets *de jure* or *de facto* priorities for domestic issues are in operation.

Germany is the only European country in which the issue of foreign securities is completely free of any restrictions. In fact such issues actually enjoy fiscal concessions not extended to domestic issues. Germany has an embarrassingly large export surplus available for lending. But owing to the high interest rates on domestic issues that prevailed until recently, and also to borrowers' fears that the D. mark might be revalued, the extent to which this freedom led to actual German long-term lending abroad was before 1968 relatively small. Although restrictions were relaxed in France in 1967, they had to be reimposed next year. Nevertheless, French banks participate actively in international syndicates engaged in issuing Euro-bonds, and loans to countries of the Franc Area are often authorised.

In Britain the ban on foreign issues is selective. Exceptions have been made in favour of loans to Sterling Area and EFTA countries, also in favour of refunding loans and of loans the proceeds of which are spent in the U.K. Above all, the issue of foreign loans is free if subscriptions are limited to non-residents, or to residents paying with investment currencies. Licenses are granted to investment trusts and other institutional investors to invest in approved foreign securities.

In Belgium authorisation by the Finance Ministry is required for foreign issues and such authorisation is liable to be refused for various reasons. In the Netherlands foreign issues are permitted up to a maximum annual total and they are subject to other limitations. In Switzerland the authorities adapt their attitude to changes in the balance of payments. There is usually a long queue of would-be foreign borrowers in the Swiss market. In Italy foreign issues are subject to Government authorisation.

There is now far too much domestic official borrowing in most capital markets. In London and in other centres such borrowing takes up a very high proportion of the available capital resources.

Taxes imposed on new issues and on transfers of securities are considerably higher than before the war. In Britain the stamp duty on new issues of bearer bonds is 2 per cent, in Belgium 1·6 per cent, in Italy it varies according to the nominal amount of the bonds. In France and Luxembourg there is no duty. In Germany there is a 2½ per cent tax. The duty on transfers of bonds was reduced in Britain in 1963 from 2 to 1 per cent, in Belgium it is 0·24 per cent, in France 0·6 per cent for spot transactions and 0·3 per cent for forward transactions. In Italy there is a ½ per cent annual tax on bonds in circulation and a nominal transfer duty. This list indicates the existence of wide discrepancies between the taxation on foreign bonds. In almost every instance the taxes are higher than before the war, but they are far from being prohibitive. Other costs associated with capital issues have also been increased though not disproportionately compared with the general trend of money values. They are much higher in London than in New York and much higher on the Continent than in London.

Taxation of investment incomes and of capital gains has increased considerably everywhere. The latter has been introduced in countries where it did not exist before the war. It tends to discourage taking risks, owing to the inadequacy of reward in the form of taxed yield and of capital profits. But in this respect, too, the situation is not intolerable.

Post-war monetary policy, especially in Britain, interfered from time to time with issuing activity in general to a much larger extent than in the old days, because, in addition to having to iron out booms and slumps, it has to protect the exchange and the gold reserve. This affects foreign bond issues particularly. The balance of payments position changed against foreign lending in London and during the 'sixties also against unrestricted lending in New York. The two main pre-war long-term lenders, Britain and the United States, are now burdened with a very large amount of foreign short-term indebtedness. This reduces their pre-war capacity of overlending because, amidst the changed currency situation, it involves considerable risks. The rôle played by the pound and the dollar as reserve currencies has greatly curtailed the freedom of the two countries to issue foreign loans. The country which, at the time of writing, seems to be in the best position to lend abroad owing to its perennial export surplus is Germany.

Devaluation and revaluation fears affect facilities for foreign loans to a much larger extent than those for domestic capital issues. In respect of the latter, borrowers and lenders have the same currency, so that the problem does not present itself in such an acute form as in the case of foreign loans where one of the parties has to take an exchange risk.

Foreign exchange markets for the use of foreign borrowers are quite satisfactory. There are now also ample short-term investment facilities at the disposal of foreign borrowers to employ their unspent balances profitably. The Euro-currency markets are used very extensively for that purpose.

It is clear from the above survey that, on balance, the conditions required for the issue of foreign loans are now not nearly as adequate as before the war. Countries which have adequate export surpluses do not possess the necessary mechanism, or their investors are not interested sufficiently in foreign loans, or there are exchange restrictions. Demand for capital runs high and exceeds supply, hence high interest rates. The prospects of a gradual depreciation of the monetary units of loans and the competition of equities for the capital available for investment contribute towards the high interest rates on straight bonds. As pointed out above, a compromise has been found in the issue of convertible bonds.

For a long time New York was able to satisfy the high post-war demand for loans by creditworthy countries. London, although well equipped for lending abroad, was prevented from doing so by the priority given to direct investment abroad. The extent to which Continental markets were able to participate was until recently relatively limited. Nor was there a satisfactroy progress towards the integration of the capital markets of the European Economic Community. The conclusion which emerged from these facts was that, in order to provide an alternative market to New York, an integration of the capital issuing activities of London and of the leading Western European centres was essential.

CHAPTER FIVE

Entrepôt for International Capital

THE rule that a country's ability to lend its domestic savings to foreign borrowers depends in the long run on the existence of an export surplus need not necessarily mean that countries without an export surplus are absolutely precluded from lending to foreign borrowers. A country which has substantial reserves may be prepared to lend abroad during periods when it has no export surplus, on the assumption that before very long it would have a surplus. Or it may be able to lend money borrowed from abroad, or re-borrow money lent in the absence of an export surplus, without subjecting its balance of payments to undue strain. There is a strong case for performing such a function if the financial centre concerned possesses banks which inspire confidence abroad and have good international connections in addition to having an efficient mechanism for handling such transactions – always provided that the economy of the country is basically sound, so that the assumption that the reappearance of export surpluses is a mere question of time is well-founded.

We saw in the last chapter that the capacity of capital markets to meet the demand for foreign loans has declined in most respects more or less, compared with the pre-1914 period and with the active periods between the wars. Even New York came to be affected by perennial balance of payments difficulties during the 'sixties. By 1963 the United States became very anxious to divert from New York some of the foreign long-term borrowing and to encourage European markets to relieve New York of a large part of the burden which the dollar could no longer carry. But since each European market was in some way handicapped and could not replace New York to any extent, it became necessary for them to combine somehow their facilities in order to be able to relieve the dollar of the pressure due to overlending.

Had Britain joined the Common Market the integration of London's facilities for foreign capital issues with those of other European financial centres would have provided the answer to the problem. As it was, the European centres concerned had to learn by experience that they were unable to take up the loans that the United States Government diverted from New York, without London's active participation, indeed without London's lead. But it was equally obvious that Britain was not in a position to replace the United States as a provider of capital for foreign borrowers. Her balance of payments position and her reserve position were incomparably worse than those of the United States. It is true, her balance of payments deficit, as that of the United States, was largely due to over-exporting capital through direct investment. But the United States had a reasonably satisfactory balance of visible trade and in possession of a large if declining gold reserve she was in an incomparably stronger position to stand the strain. In spite of her heavy gold losses, she could afford to lose more, even though it was becoming increasingly obvious that the drain could not continue indefinitely. For Britain even a relatively moderate aggravation of the pressure on sterling as a result of foreign loans might have meant an acute crisis.

A solution had to be found enabling London to resume its international banking rôle in the sphere of long-term lending without thereby aggravating the pressure on sterling. The solution lay in the adoption of the rôle of an entrepôt for foreign capital – that is, lending to foreign borrowers capital owned by non-resident investors.

Addressing the annual dinner given by the Lord Mayor of London to bankers and merchants of the City of London on 3 October 1962, the Governor of the Bank of England, Lord Cromer, declared: 'The time has now come when the City once again might provide an international capital market where the foreigner cannot only borrow long-term capital where . . .

will once again wish to place his long-term placement capital. This entrepôt business in capital . . . would not only fill a vital and vacant rôle in Europe in mobilising foreign capital for world economic development. It would be to the advantage of British industry in financing our customers.'

Lord Cromer's remark did not indicate the method by which London should, in his opinion, fulfil the rôle of entrepôt of capital. In a sense London, like practically every other international financial centre, has always fulfilled that rôle to a large extent. It has acted as an entrepôt mostly by re-lending to foreign borrowers foreign deposits and other foreign funds held in the form of short-term investments, but also by re-lending foreign long-term capital invested in Britain in the form of holdings of British securities and in other forms of long-term investment.

A strong financial centre attracts foreign funds. Unless the equivalent of these funds is kept in the form of additional gold or official foreign exchange reserves, or is spent on additional imports, it automatically assumes the form of an increase in the short-term claims of the country concerned against other countries. Conversely, if a country overlends, unless the excess is paid for in the form of gold export or a reduction of the official reserve, or through a curtailment of imports or increase of exports, it is automatically re-borrowed through a corresponding increase of the country's foreign short-term liabilities.

In any active international financial centre there are constant flows of foreign capital in both directions, inward as well as outward. To the extent to which the amounts lent abroad and borrowed abroad are balanced the financial centre does fulfil the rôle of entrepôt for foreign capital. This does not necessarily mean that the individual institutions engaged in that transaction actually fulfil that part. Any one bank may be concerned only with lending abroad or only with borrowing abroad. What matters is that the financial centre or the country as a whole re-lends the amount borrowed or re-borrows the amount lent. In many instances the same banks both lend and borrow abroad, but they need not borrow abroad for the purpose of lending abroad. It just happens to work out that way.

London has long enjoyed the confidence of foreign countries and many foreign investors have long been in the habit of holding substantial amounts of securities in addition to holding sterling deposits and short-term investments. London re-lent these amounts – or, to be exact, amounts corresponding to those received, to foreign borrowers. Germany between the wars pursued the practice of borrowing abroad on short-term for the purpose of re-lending to Soviet Russia and other countries on long-term. In doing so she too performed the functions of an entrepôt for foreign capital. That rôle was per-formed even more distinctly by New York before the war. A very high proportion of dollar bonds issued there during the 'twenties found their way back to the borrowing countries or to other foreign countries. Moreover, citizens and institutions of countries borrowing from the United States invested in American securities or lent to Wall Street. What happened was that the United States re-borrowed part of the amounts lent abroad. This is what happened also in more recent times.

The Latin American countries, while borrowing abroad, also exported capital in the form of refugee funds owned by their citizens. The Soviet Union, too, is an active entrepôt of capital, having secured Government-guaranteed long-term credits of £100 million from Britian and promptly re-lending to Egypt an identical amount.

What Lord Cromer had in mind was something quite different from any of these practices. He envisaged the issue of foreign loans in London without the participation of British capital even in the form of re-lending borrowed foreign capital in such transactions. There is no question of re-borrowing or re-lending of foreign capital. London bankers are neither lenders nor borrowers, their function is confined to placing foreign bonds with foreign investors.

It is true, the London issuing houses and the underwriters may finance the transactions temporarily, pending the definite placing of the bonds with investors abroad. It is also true that

British investors in foreign securities are also in a position to acquire the newly issued foreign bonds if they realise their investments in order to secure the investment dollars required, or if they acquire such investment dollars from other former British holders of foreign securities. But in substance such transactions simply amount to turning over existing foreign investment. No additional British capital is lent abroad. London is merely acting as intermediary between foreign borrowers and foreign investors, and the latter provide all the capital lent by London. Or, the foreign securities are acquired by U.K. residents from other U.K. residents.

U.K. residents are not in a position to take up bonds, apart from institutional investors specially authorised to do so. For this reason alone, the requirements of such a market for new issues differ materially in many respects both from those of a capital market for domestic borrowers and from those of a capital market which lends local capital or borrowed foreign capital to foreign borrowers.

Most foreign loans issued in London during 1963–69 were in U.S. dollars, though a number of them were in terms of other currencies or in composite units of account. We saw earlier that a few loans were issued in terms of sterling, but they were for repayment of maturing sterling loans. Some sterling loans were also made to countries of the Sterling Area or to EFTA countries. In some instances the issues were made in sterling with dollars or D. mark as the alternative currency, but such issues were subject to the same restrictions as other loans in terms of foreign currencies – U.K. residents were only permitted to subscribe with the aid of investment currencies.

The issue of foreign bonds in foreign currency denominations does not necessarily mean that the rôle of the issuing centre is confined to that of an entrepôt for capital. We saw earlier that many international loans issued during the 'twenties in terms of sterling or dollars had tranches issued in Holland or Switzerland, which countries were fully prepared to take up bonds in denominations of foreign currencies. In our days, too, residents in many countries are entitled to acquire and hold bonds in terms of a foreign currency. The issuing centre assumes the rôle of an entrepôt, in the sense in which the term was employed by Lord Cromer, if residents do not acquire such bonds in circumstances in which the transaction would entail a net export of capital, and the whole amount of the capital lent to foreign borrowers is contributed by non-residents. This need not necessarily mean that the amount lent is capital newly exported by foreign countries. A great many subscribers may pay for the bonds with the aid of sterling held on non-resident account which the holders are of course entitled to invest wherever they like. This again does not entail an export of British capital. What happens is that sterling which is already in foreign hands is lent to other foreign residents.

The differences between the requirements of an international capital market in which local capital is lent and one which serves as an entrepôt for foreign capital may be summarised as follows.

(1) There is no need for such a capital market to possess plentiful supplies of local savings in excess of local requirements of capital.

(2) The attitude of local investors towards foreign investments is of no great importance.

(3) There is no need for the country in which the foreign loans are issued to have a balance of payment surplus.

(4) It is immaterial if the local currency is subject to devaluation or revaluation rumours, since it is not the currency in terms of which the loans are issued.

(5) The currency of the loan contract, on the other hand, must not be suspected of being likely to be revalued or devalued.

(6) Exchange restrictions affecting the local currency are a disadvantage, but unless they also affect transactions between non-residents they do not prevent foreign issuing activity or the development of secondary markets.

(7) It is an advantage, though not of decisive importance, if the financial centre has a good market in Euro-dollars and other Euro-currencies.

(8) It is an advantage, though not of decisive importance, if local residents are in a position to subscribe with the aid of investment dollars or currencies of a similar type.

(9) The foreign bonds issued should be listed on Stock Exchanges both in the issuing centres and elsewhere.

(10) Above all, it is essential that the issuing banks should have good connections with banks and investors abroad.

Since loans in terms of foreign currencies are issued primarily for non-resident investors – apart from resident investors who want to switch their foreign investments or who replace other U.K. investors – the supply of local capital is immaterial. Generally speaking, however, confidence in a financial centre presupposes adequacy of financial resources. It has proved to be possible for a country that is a persistent net borrower abroad to fulfil the rôle of an entrepôt for foreign capital. What matters more is that the country in which bonds are placed by the issuing houses of the entrepôt centre should possess adequate financial resources for that purpose.

For the above reason, the attitude of local investors is of no decisive importance. Nevertheless, since many of the large institutional investors in the country that issues the loan play the part of underwriters, their attitude is not a matter of indifference. Moreover, subscriptions with the aid of investment currencies may in given circumstances contribute marginally to the success of the issues.

As already remarked, there is no need for a country acting as entrepôt for foreign capital to have a balance of payments surplus. But a substantial perennial balance of payments deficit might in the long run undermine confidence in the financial centre concerned. In order that a centre should be able to continue to function as an entrepôt for capital, it is not essential for its currency to be absolutely above suspicion in the sense of being neither devaluation-prone nor revaluation-prone. If, however, there are acute waves of distrust their psychological effects and their disturbing effects on Euro-bond prices might introduce elements of complications. In given circumstances issuing houses and underwriters might be inclined to limit their commitments.

What matters more is that the currency of the contract should not be suspect. It is all to the good if that currency is not suspected by borrowers of being revaluation-prone or by lenders of being devaluation-prone. The ideal solution is to select a currency which is hard but not too hard. During the 'sixties the dollar met those requirements, which accounts for the fact that, in spite of the progress made by the D. mark, the large majority of Euro-bond issues are still in terms of dollars.

The country in which the bonds are issued need not be entirely free of exchange restrictions, but those in force must not apply to non-residents. Above all, the currency of the loan contract must not be restricted for non-residents. It is essential that they should be able to transfer the proceeds of their Euro-bonds at any time at current exchange rates. It is also important that they should be at liberty to employ their balances on non-resident account in the entrepôt centre for subscribing to or buying bonds issued in the market concerned.

We saw in the previous chapter that availability of short-term credit facilities is an essential condition of a good capital market. This applies equally to markets acting as entrepôt; they are in need of Euro-dollar and other Euro-currency facilities, or other forms of short-term credit, for the temporary financing of their bond issues.

Even though the rôle of entrepôt implies the placing of the foreign bonds abroad, it helps if issuing houses can depend on being able to place at least some of them locally. For this reason it is an advantage if the special exchange rate at which local residents are entitled to acquire currencies required for paying for foreign bonds is not at too heavy a premium against the ordinary exchange rate.

It is essential for the bonds to be listed not only on the Stock Exchange of the issuing centre but also on one or several Stock Exchanges abroad. It is a particular advantage if they can be listed on the Stock Exchange of the country in whose currency the bonds are issued, which is the reason why many

European dollar bonds issues are listed in Wall Street, even if there is no present demand for them. But this is not an indispensable condition. It helps a great deal if the issuing houses have branches or affiliates in countries where they want to place the bonds. This is probably one of the reasons why several London banking houses have opened branches or affiliates abroad in recent years. The issuing houses must have good clients among investors abroad, especially among those possessing non-resident sterling or Euro-currency deposits in London.

The creation and maintenance of an entrepôt for foreign capital entails considerable advantages. The advantages to borrowers are obvious, especially if a situation arises in which a financial centre with ample experience and efficient technical organisation for foreign issues is prevented by its balance of payments position from lending its domestic capital or from re-lending borrowed capital, and if centres with ample resources available for lending do not possess the necessary technical organisation or are prevented from lending abroad by institutional inhibitions. From the point of view of the country acting as entrepôt the advantages are not confined to the invisible exports represented by the commissions earned on the transactions. As likely as not the proceeds of the loans may be employed by the borrowers for buying goods in the country of the entrepôt centre. The issuing houses are enabled to recover and maintain their technique which might become rusty if the balance of payments position of their country prevents them over a prolonged period from keeping up their practice by issuing loans taken up by local investors.

Above all, the possibility of acting as entrepôt for foreign capital enables the market playing that rôle to co-operate closely with markets possessing ample capital resources and a favourable balance of payments. This is essential from the point of view of achieving an integration in European capital markets. Kindleberger pointed out in an article appearing in the *Weltwirtsdaftliches Archiv* in 1963 that eight years after the conclusion of the Treaty of Rome there was no integration

C

between the capital markets of the six EEC countries. Within a few months after this observation was published the reappearance of London as a lender, in spite of the fact that its rôle was confined to that of an entrepôt, has resulted in a remarkable progress towards the integration of the European capital markets, in the complete absence of any progress towards an integration of E.E.C. capital markets.

CHAPTER SIX

The Market in Euro-Bonds

ALTHOUGH the post-war practice of foreign long-term lending in the form of dollar bonds issued in Europe developed in Continental centres already during the late 'fifties, not until London came to take an active hand in 1963 did it come to assume really considerable proportions. On the Continental markets part of the foreign issuing activity assumed the form of bonds in terms of their respective local currencies. In particular, foreign loans were issued in Germany in terms of D. marks and in Switzerland in terms of Swiss francs. Although it was technically possible for London to issue foreign loans for non-residents in terms of sterling, the dollar was chosen in preference to sterling in all but the few instances mentioned in the last chapter – loans to the Sterling Area, to EFTA countries and for re-financing. There were also a few other foreign loans issued in terms of sterling which offered the choice between sterling and D. marks or dollars. Most of the foreign loans were issued either in terms of dollars or in terms of composite units of account, mostly the former.

We saw in Chapter 4 that since the war the ability of each of the Continental financial centres to issue foreign loans has been, for various reasons, limited, and that it would have been clearly beyond their resources to handle the entire volume of additional loans diverted from New York as a result of announcement of the Interest Equalisation Tax. It was, therefore, essential that London should participate once more in foreign capital issuing activity, even if British residents remained precluded by exchange restrictions from active participation in such loans. In fact during the five years that followed the announcement of the Interest Equalisation Tax, London assumed the lead for the issue of foreign dollar bonds.

No data are available about London's participation in the various loans which were issued partly in other countries. As these loans were not offered to the public the respective amounts of the participations of various members of the consortium did not have to be published, though many prospectuses did volunteer that information. In any case, it was immaterial how much of the total the London members of the consortium handled, because even London's share was placed with investors outside the United Kingdom. What mattered was that in the majority of issues of dollar bonds in which London participated some London issuing house headed the consortium. By implication Continental banks accepted London's lead in these international transactions. This in spite of the fact that the British investors' rôle in taking up these dollar bonds was necessarily very limited.

Theoretically it was possible for U.K. residents to subscribe to such loans either through acquiring investment dollars in the market or through switching their existing dollar investments. In recent years the high premium discouraged subscriptions through buying investment dollars. Conceivably in some situations it might have appeared convenient for British holders of dollar securities to switch into newly issued dollar bonds, but the volume of such operations could not have represented more than a fraction of the issue. On the other hand, there is a fair scope for investing in such bonds the reserves and pension funds of British subsidiaries abroad. This is understood to have been done in fact on a fairly considerable scale. Even so, it must represent a minor part of the total dollar bond issued through London. The bulk of the capital raised here came from non-resident accounts or Euro-currency in London or from accounts of foreign investors with banks in other countries.

London is one of the four main international centres for refugee funds in the broadest sense, the other three being New York, Frankfurt and Switzerland. London banks handle a large number of accounts for non-residents who keep their funds here for a variety of reasons. Funds on these accounts may have the legal status of non-resident sterling, or they may be

Euro-dollar or other Euro-currency accounts. Holders of such accounts may find it advantageous in given circumstances to invest in Euro-bonds. Many foreign clients of London banks may pay for the bonds with the aid of foreign balances held on their behalf in foreign centres. Many British residents abroad who are in contact with London banks are potential investors in Euro-bonds. Some of the more active London issuing houses have a long list of clients over the five continents and advise them about forthcoming issues.

Even so, London banks would not be able to handle large amounts of Euro-bond issues unless they were associated in the transaction with overseas banks. On the published announcement of the sale of bonds there are usually the names of one or more London and New York issuing houses and those of Continental countries, including banks in the borrowing countries. This latter fact indicates that part of the Euro-bond issues is usually taken up by investors in the borrowing countries themselves. The arrangement provides a convenient formula under which the Governments concerned can borrow from their own nationals in terms of dollars or of other currencies without suffering loss of face for issuing a domestic loan in terms of a foreign currency. In certain situations investors in the borrowing country trust the borrower's solvency while distrusting the local currency. Or they may prefer bonds issued in some leading financial centre.

If the composition of the consortium for Euro-bond issues is international, that of the underwriting syndicate is even more so. It often includes banks in most Western European countries and also some banks outside Europe. They participate in each others' issues on the basis of reciprocity. New York banks, too, participate increasingly in the European issues.

Some loans are placed firmly in advance of their formal issue, while others are unloaded by the issuing houses or underwriters gradually. None of the Euro-bonds that are issued in London are offered for subscription to the public, for the simple reason that, apart from the exceptions indicated above, U.K. residents are not in a position to apply. Many Continental issues on the

other hand, are available for the rank and file of local investors.
Sub-underwriting is usually taken by many insurance companies, investment trusts, Stock Exchange firms, etc., who are
prepared to retain for themselves or for their clients the bonds
they have to take up or who definitely take over their bonds or
sub-underwriting terms.

There is no restriction on the acquisition of dollar bonds by
residents in Western Germany or in Switzerland. Indeed in
Germany such issues are not subject to the 25 per cent tax on
domestic issues acquired by foreign residents. French residents
were until 1968 free to buy foreign securities, but foreign issues
were not authorised. In any case portfolio investments abroad
are surrounded by measures of strict Government supervision
of the kind that is disliked by French investors. In Holland
and Belgium investors can only subscribe with the aid of
investment currencies similar to British investment dollars, but
since the premium on such investment currencies is kept down
by official intervention to a very low figure in practice this is no
obstacle to local subscription. Indeed the very existence of a
remote possibility that the Dutch or Belgium authorities might
discontinue their support of the respective investment currencies in their countries provides an inducement for the acquisition
of dollar bonds and other foreign securities by local residents.
For if, as a result of a suspension of the official support, the
premium on investment currencies should widen, Dutch or
Belgian holders of foreign securities would stand to benefit by
it when they realise their holdings and the proceeds of their
holdings.

Foreign funds on accounts with banks in Switzerland or
elsewhere, especially accumulated Middle East oil royalties, are
potential sources of investment in Euro-bonds. So are refugee
funds from every part of the world deposited in any financial
centre. Once they are outside their countries of origin, exchange
controls applied either at home or abroad can not prevent their
owners from acquiring Euro-bonds. Since principal and interest
can be made payable, at the bondholders' option, in the United
States or in the country where there is a paying agent, the bonds

are convenient investment for holders of refugee funds who trust the dollar or, as the case may be, the D. mark or some other currency.

Judging by the large number of such issues, the market for them must have a substantial capacity. After each run of such issues it is usually suggested that 'saturation point' was reached. But before very long further issues appeared and were easily absorbed by investors.

Countries for whose benefits Euro-bonds have been issued include Japan, Denmark, Norway, Finland, Italy, Portugal, Austria, France, Belgium, the U.S., the U.K. and Israel. Borrowers include Governments, Government-controlled industrial and other concerns, public utiltiies, municipal authorities, insurance companies, banks, and private industrial and commercial concerns. International institutions figure prominently among borrowers. The loans issued by corporations often assume the form of convertible debentures.

A number of five-year notes have been issued. The bonds are repayable mostly between ten and twenty years and their interest varies mostly between 6½ and 7½ per cent. They are usually issued a shade under par. They are not secured as a rule by any specific security, but in many instances they are Government-guaranteed, or the Central Bank concerned gives an undertaking to provide the currency required for the service of the loans. In this latter respect the terms vary considerably according to the view the issuing houses take about the need for safeguarding bondholders against future exchange control measures.

Several early Danish issues, for instance, contained a clause according to which the borrower will be authorised under Danish legislation and regulations *now in force*, to purchase the dollars required for the loan service. Evidently such a clause does not safeguard bondholders against a possible future reinforcement of exchange control. An early issue of the Istituto per la Ricostruzione Industriale – a corporation owned by the Italian Government – contains a similarly inadequate clause which does not prevent the Government from blocking the transfer of interest and principal by simply changing the law. On the other hand, the prospectus of a Finnish issue contained a paragraph stating that the Bank of Finland has 'confirmed in writing that it will authorise before the due dates the free transfer of the U.S. dollars required for the service of the Bond Certificates'. A Portuguese Government loan contains an even more watertight provision: 'The Republic of Portugal undertakes to transfer or make available all funds required for the service of the Bonds . . . in U.S. dollars under all circumstances without any limitations and outside any bilateral or multilateral payments or clearing agreement to which the Republic of Portugal may be a party at the times these payments are made.'

Such a watertight formula should be applied to all loan contracts. Failing that it should be made plain that the Government of the borrowers reserve the right to suspend at any time the transfer of the dollars for the debt service. Investors who are prepared to take that risk should be enabled to do so with their eyes open. It is true, in the case of some countries, the risk of future exchange control is not nearly so grave as in the case of others. Even so, as the situation in that respect is liable to change suddenly, issuing houses should deem it their duty to secure for their clients the largest possible measure of safeguards.

Since none of the Governments concerned appear to have had any objection to safeguarding bondholders against deduction of taxes, *present or future*, there could be no logical reason for withholding similar safeguards in respect of future exchange control.

The payment of interest and principal is 'in U.S. dollars in the form of a transfer to a bank in the United States or of a dollar cheque paid in the United States, subject to the regulations in the country of the recipient'. This clause appears in practically every loan contract, and its only variation is for loans which are payable also in other currencies, for which similar provisions are inserted in respect of payment in those currencies.

Euro-bonds are listed on a number of Stock Exchanges,

including the Luxembourg *bourse* where there are special fiscal and other concessions to attract foreign issues. Inasmuch as dollar bonds are often payable in New York and are deposited there, they are also listed on the New York Stock Exchange.

But we shall see in the next chapter that transactions in Euro-bonds are concluded mostly outside Stock Exchanges. In this respect the system is somewhat similar to that of foreign dollar bonds that had been issued in New York – they still are issued for countries to which the Interest Equalisation Tax does not apply – dealings in which are not in Wall Street but between banks or with customers 'over the counter'. One of the reasons for this is that spreads between buying and selling quotations for such bonds are often too narrow to allow for the cost of transactions through Stock Exchanges.

All Euro-bonds are bearer bonds. In order to encourage transactions in London the war-time exchange control measure banning the issue of bearer bonds has been repealed. The bonds are free of any withholding tax.

There is very active arbitrage in Euro-bonds between various centres. Firms specialising in such transactions take advantage of discrepancies between the various quotations of the same securities in different centres, also of discrepancies that are liable to develop between prices of bonds which are comparable – for instance between Norwegian and Danish municipal issues.

Switzerland is prominent among subscribers or subsequent purchasers of Euro-bonds. Most of the bonds are believed to have been acquired not for Swiss investors but for foreign holders of accounts with Swiss banks.

A question which is often asked but is seldom answered is, what is the absorbing capacity of the Euro-bond market? As pointed out earlier, every now and again it is widely believed that saturation point has been reached. But in this respect, as in several other respects, the history of Euro-currencies seems to have repeated itself. On a great many occasions during the 'sixties financial commentators contended that the expansion of the Euro-dollar market had passed its peak. If we took the trouble to count the number of such pronouncements we would find that the Euro-dollar market had more 'peaks' than the whole range of the Himalaya. In a similar way, it was asserted again and again that there was no more room for Euro-bond issues. Yet after each occasion the market and the investors managed to digest the issues and after a while it was possible to proceed with new issues.

In examining the question of absorbing capacity we must distinguish between the absorbing capacity of issuing houses and underwriters and that of ultimate holders. In 1968 the question did not arise, because most issues were oversubscribed in advance. In less booming conditions it takes time for banks to place the bonds and the financial mechanism engaged in the task is apt to become clogged with ill-digested issues. What matters is whether they can be unloaded in a short time, making room for the next issue. When the absorbing capacity of investors becomes exhausted – as it did in 1965–66 and during the rise in interest rates in 1969 – issuing activity must slow down until new capital becomes available. Natural accumulation of savings replace the funds invested, but if most investors who are interested in that type of investment become pessimistic about price prospects increases in resources need not in itself make necessarily room for more issues. What is needed then is the tapping of new markets. Bonds have to be made attractive to new types of investors by changing their terms or their type.

A substantial increase in the absorbing capacity of the market for Euro-bonds may occur through the following causes:

(1) Additional refugee funds may become available. For instance, the flight of Italian capital to Switzerland in the middle 'sixties and the flight of French capital to Germany and Switzerland in 1968 provided additional funds for investment in Euro-bonds. War scars in the Middle East are apt to make more funds available.

(2) The dollar may become more attractive to investors through becoming harder because of an improvement in the balance of payments of the United States, or the

adoption of deflationary policies, or a termination of hostilities in the Far East, etc.

(3) Other currencies, such as the D. mark at the time of writing, may become more attractive to potential investors in Euro-bonds.

(4) Government measures may divert capital from alternative forms of investment. For instance, the imposition of the 25 per cent tax in Germany on domestic securities held by non-residents induced many holders to switch into Euro-bonds.

(5) Relaxation of exchange control in the issuing countries or in the investing countries would enable residents in these countries to invest in Euro-bonds.

(6) Decline in the premium on investment dollars and other similar currencies would make it worth while for residents in the countries concerned to acquire Euro-bonds with the aid of such currencies.

(7) Inhibitions which prevent institutional investors from investing in such types of securities might be relaxed.

On the other hand, the absorbing capacity of the market is liable to contract for the following reasons:

(1) Repatriation of refugee funds – such as occurred in France after the settlement of the Algerian problem – might entail disinvestment in the Euro-bond market.

(2) Confidence in the dollar might weaken, without a simultaneous increase of confidence in some other currency, for instance if an all-round devaluation of currencies is expected.

(3) United States Government measures diverting long-term borrowing from New York to other markets might be mitigated or reversed.

(4) A rise in interest rates would discourage demand for straight bonds, while a fall in equities would discourage demand for convertible bonds.

(5) Exchange control measures might be reinforced and the investors affected might be prevented from acquiring or holding Euro-bonds.

The above list is by no means exhaustive and there is an ever-present possibility of unexpected changes in the absorbing capacity of the market. As far as issuing houses and under-writers are concerned, their absorbing capacity is also open to changes, but ultimately it depends on that of investors.

CHAPTER SEVEN

The Secondary Market

THE prospects of a further expansion of the Euro-bond market depend not only on its absorbing capacity for new issues but also on the expansion of a secondary market – or after-market, as it is called sometimes – that enables investors to buy or sell Euro-bonds when it is convenient to them and on reasonable terms. In the absence of a good secondary market, only those investors would take up new issues who intend to keep them until maturity or who are prepared to risk having to realise their holdings in an inadequate market at unfavourable prices. Since a large proportion of potential subscribers to new issues would be reluctant to subscribe without the assurance provided by the existence of a good secondary market, the absorbing capacity of the Euro-issue market would remain relatively limited without a good secondary market.

Largely for this very reason, for some time after its emergence, the Euro-issue market did in fact remain rather limited. The absence of an adequate secondary market explains to a high degree why issuing activity came to a halt from time to time because the market became easily congested. It was not until the late 'sixties that an increasingly active secondary market came to develop, and this made it possible to increase the volume of new issues considerably.

Because an active secondary market is now in existence, a large and increasing number of investors all over the world are no more willing to subscribe to new issues and also to buy bonds issued earlier. This makes it easier for investors who want to dispose of their holdings to find a counterpart at reasonable current market prices. It enables members of issuing groups and underwriters to unload gradually bonds which could not be placed with investors immediately.

The secondary market assumes the form of active dealing between financial houses ready to sell or buy Euro-bonds on their own accounts, to or from each other and to or from their clients. This task has always been performed by Stock Exchanges, and it had been originally assumed that a number of local markets would be created in Euro-bonds mainly on the various Stock Exchanges by which the bonds were listed. But from this point of view the progress of the Euro-bond market has been disappointing. The volume of turnover in most Euro-bonds on most Stock Exchanges is relatively small, and dealings are few and far between. A much higher proportion of the bonds change hands between financial houses most of which are not members of Stock Exchanges, or between these financial houses and their clients 'over the counter' – to employ a not strictly accurate but widely used term – both locally and internationally.

One of the reasons why dealings with Euro-bonds on Stock Exchanges have failed to expand in accordance with the increase in the volume of buying and selling of Euro-bonds after their issue lies in the multiplicity of relatively small loans and their fragmentation through issuing or subsequently selling bonds of each issue in a number of countries. The amount of a great many issues does not exceed $20 million, so that holdings in each country participating in any one of such issue or acquiring the bonds subsequently amount to barely a few millions of dollars. This is not sufficient to give rise to an active turnover on the Stock Exchange of any one of the countries concerned. Since the issues are essentially international their secondary markets, too, have to be essentially international in order to ensure a reasonably large turnover in which buying and selling orders can easily be matched. This fundamental requirement is fulfilled by the secondary market that has developed between dealers in Euro-bonds outside Stock Exchanges, who do not confine their operations to other dealers in their respective financial centres. There is now a very active international turnover in a large and increasing number of Euro-bonds. While a high proportion of many issues is held firmly by the original subscribers, others change hands quite frequently.

If a bank or a financial house receives a buying or selling order from one of its customers, and if it is not an active participant in the secondary market, it places an order with a house which is an active participant. Many banks combine the function of managing issues, participating in issuing syndicates and underwriting Euro-bonds with the functions of dealing in them in the after-market. There is no strict division of labour between those engaged in these distinct functions, though usually only large banks are managers.

When a house participating in the secondary market receives a buying or selling order, either from a client or from another bank, it does not act as an intermediary but provides the counterpart on its own account. The next step is to cover the transaction in the market, unless it happens to be able to 'marry' buying and selling orders, or unless it chooses to let the transaction change its own commitments in the Euro-bond concerned. Otherwise it will try to undo its commitment by buying from or selling to a dealer, if possible locally. If a counterpart is not available locally on acceptable terms it contacts dealers in other centres. Dealing between centres is usually so active – or at any rate quotations are asked for and given so frequently – that the whole of Western Europe may be considered to constitute one single market. The turnover in that international market is estimated to average some $50 million a day at the time of writing, and on many days the number of transactions are believed to exceed a thousand.

Some dealers specialise in a number of bonds or in certain types of bonds, in respect of which they play the same part as is played by jobbers on the London Stock Exchange. They quote simultaneously buying and selling rates and are prepared to deal either way on their own account. The spread between the two rates varies and is liable to change according to the trend of the market or the trend in particular bonds. Broadly speaking it ranges from $\frac{1}{8}$ point to $\frac{1}{2}$ point. Thanks to active international dealing, banks wanting to buy or sell bonds for their clients or for their own account can usually depend on being able to find a counterpart without difficulty and at prices which correspond to a reasonable degree to supply-demand relationship of the moment. Owing to the number of active dealers who are prepared to have a position in bonds in which they are interested, the market has become quite efficient and tends to become progressively more efficient.

Participants in this market need never meet in the flesh. They communicate with each other by private telephone lines in the same market and by long-distance telephone calls or by teleprinter between markets. From this point of view its mechanism bears much closer resemblance to foreign exchange markets or to Euro-currency markets than to conventional bond markets on Stock Exchanges. But a much more important difference between the Euro-bond market and dealings in foreign bonds on Stock Exchanges is the essentially international character of the secondary market. Some Stock Exchange firms, too, engage in international transactions, but members of the secondary market are in much closer contact with their trading partners abroad. Of course stockbroker firms, too, can be members of the secondary market.

The secondary market embraces also New York to the extent to which the United States can participate as an intermediary in transactions on account of non-residents, and also other centres outside Europe, especially Tokyo, Hong Kong, Beirut, Caracas, etc. There are markets in some borrowing countries, too, not only for new issues but also for existing bonds.

An important handicap to the expansion of the secondary markets – and for that matter to the expansion of the Euro-issue market in general – is the existence of discrepancies between practices, rules, taxation, etc. Such discrepancies complicate Euro-bond transactions. The principal houses engaged in the secondary market formed an association in 1969 to elaborate proposals aiming at a higher degree of uniformity in practices. This would go some way towards reducing delays in the delivery of bonds sold in the secondary market. Towards the end of 1968 it amounted to anything up to two or three months.

This tended to discourage dealing — one of the leading American houses actually suspended undertaking new transactions until it could catch up with arrears of delivery – and indirectly also the issue of new loans, even though there were no comparable delays in the delivery of newly-issued bonds to subscribers. Apart from the complications arising from the discrepancies referred to above, the main cause of delays is shortage of clerical staff with adequate experience in such involved operations. In particular there is a long holdup for this reason at the New York end. Even though U.S. residents are not permitted to acquire Euro-bonds, American banks play an active part in placing them with their non-resident clients. As principal and interest on Euro-bonds issued in terms of dollars is payable in New York, a great many subscribers or buyers of such bonds hold them on deposit in New York, so that in a high proportion of the transactions the bonds have to be delivered by a New York bank or to a New York bank.

To circumvent the New York 'traffic bloc' and also to speed up deliveries between European markets which are also slow, a clearing house for Euro-bonds was set up in 1968 under the auspices of the Morgan Guaranty Trust Company in Brussels under the name of 'Euro-clear'. Participants in the Euro-clear system have a securities clearance account and a dollar account with the Brussels branch of the Morgan Guaranty Trust Co. When a participant buys securities he instructs the seller to deliver it to his Brussels securities account which is credited with the securities, while his dollar account is debited with the amount payable for them. If he sells securities he instructs Euro-clear to deliver them to the buyer and the payment received is credited to his dollar account. If both parties participate in Euro-clear, the transaction can be completed by means of book entries without any physical movements of the securities or transfers of funds as between banks. If only one party participates there is no such advantage, so that the success of the scheme depends largely on its use by the largest possible number of participants.

To make the use of Euro-clear easier, arrangements have

been made to accept or make deliveries and payments also through the Frankfurt, London, New York and Paris offices of the Morgan Guaranty Company, and through associated banks in Amsterdam, Basle, Geneva, Luxembourg, Milan and Zurich. Provided that both parties participate, the arrangement saves much time even if it involves the transfer of the securities and the funds from one of the associated banks to another.

To the extent to which such clearings reduce the delays in the delivery of Euro-bonds – and also of internationally-traded dollar bonds originally issued in New York and traded in Wall Street – it would go a long way towards assisting in the further development of the market.

Thanks partly to the operation of the clearing, but even more to the temporary decline in issuing activity and in the demand on the secondary market during the spring of 1969, the delays became shorter. There are liable to increase, however with a revival of activity.

The Governments of the countries participating in the market in Euro-bonds could and should assist the market by negotiating international agreements aiming at uniformity of local regulations relating to the issue of Euro-bonds and their transfers to new holders. Of course it would be too much to expect them to achieve uniform taxation – except perhaps within trading areas such as the EEC in the course of time – but simplification of the official procedures, in addition to unification of banking and Stock Exchange practices, would be helpful.

One of the disadvantages of the absence of active dealings in Euro-bonds on Stock Exchanges is the absence of authentic quotations of their prices. Holders and would-be holders have to depend on daily and weekly lists circulated by leading houses among each other and among their clients. As any one dealer can only see a section of the markets, discrepancies between prices quoted by various houses at any given moment are liable to arise. The adoption of some system under which information about prices could be pooled and uniform lists of quotations could be published would greatly improve the secondary markets.

CHAPTER EIGHT

International Interest Rates

MY book on Euro-dollars describes and analyses the system of international short-term interest rates that has come intobeing through the development of the Euro-dollar market. This set of interest rates is distinct from, and to a large extent independent of domestic short-term interest rates either in New York or in the European financial centres where the transactions in Euro-dollars take place. The expansion of the market for Euro-bonds has applied, in a sense, this system to long-term interest rates. By 1968–69 issues of such bonds, and subsequent dealings in them, were on a sufficiently large scale to justify the contention that a level of long-term interest rates is already actually in existence. As a result of the increase in the number of Euro-bond issues and of the active and continuous turnover in the secondary market, a sort of structure of long-term interest rates and yields has emerged.

On the basis of the present volume of activity and the frequency of quotations in the Euro-bond market it is possible to discern, not only in theory but also in practice, a structure of interest rates the level of which is distinct from that emerging from the New York foreign bond market and from the foreign bond markets on the Stock Exchanges of Europe. It is of course more difficult to ascertain standard rates of interest on Euro-bonds than on Euro-currencies. As we shall propose to point out in Chapter 16 on Euro-bond price trends, in the Euro-currency market rates quoted for deposits lent to first-rate banks are fairly uniform, but in the Euro-bond market, as indeed on any bond market, interest rates and yields vary much more widely, even on straight bonds, as they depend on the borrower's standing, on the security of the loan and on other considerations. When it comes to rates for convertible bonds their terms of issue and subsequent yield depends on widely divergent influences, so that they have to be disregarded when trying to ascertain the level of international long-term interest rates. Nevertheless, interest rates on convertible bonds, as distinct from the value of their equity-content, are affected by changes in the level of interest rates on straight bonds.

Interest rates on straight dollar bonds issued for first-rate borrowers – such as, for instance, Scandinavian municipalities – was during 1968 around 6½ per cent, compared with 5½ per cent a few years earlier. The increase was not due to any deterioration of the borrowers' credit – even though the growing volume of outstanding bonds of this type may have contributed to it to some extent – but mainly to the rising trend of international long-term interest rates. During the first half of 1969 the spectacular increase in interest rates all over the world caused a further sharp increase in interest rates on Euro-bonds.

The structure of long-term international interest rates is of course not altogether independent of the interest rate structure for foreign bonds in New York or in countries where the bonds are issued or acquired, any more than Euro-dollar rates are independent of short-term rates in New York or in London. It is, of course, affected to a large extent by conditions in markets outside the United States. So long as the Interest Equalisation Tax remains in force, interest differentials in favour of Euro-bonds would have to widen very considerably before they would give rise to a sufficient demand by U.S. residents to result in an adjustment in New York quotations of European bonds that had been issued in the United States prior to the announcement of the new tax.

Nevertheless, these bonds do compete for American residents' funds which sought refuge abroad for fiscal reasons or in anticipation of future exchange restrictions in the United States. They also compete to some extent for funds owned legitimately by Americans resident abroad or by foreign subsidiaries of American firms. Decisions by holders of such funds whether or not to invest in European dollar bonds in preference to bonds issued in New York are not influenced, however, entirely by interest differentials.

Broadly speaking, the level, trend and fluctuations of international long-term interest rates is influenced (*a*) by interest rate factors, (*b*) by Stock Exchange factors, and (*c*) by foreign exchange factors. The factors liable to affect the issue terms and subsequent yields of Euro-bonds may be listed under the following headings:

(1) The amounts of Euro-bonds that are issued and their total outstanding in Europe.

(2) The degree of popularity of this type of investment among investors.

(3) The level of local long-term interest rates in countries where the bonds are issued, and in countries where they are eventually placed.

(4) The degree of liquidity of the capital markets in which the bonds are issued or placed.

(5) The views taken on the prospects of the currencies of the bonds.

(6) The views taken by investors on the prospects of their own currency.

(7) Euro-dollar or other Euro-currency deposit rates and future prospects of such rates.

(8) Forward dollar rates and other relevant forward rates if the transactions are financed with the aid of other currencies and if the exchange risk is covered.

(9) The views taken by investors on the prospects of interest rates and bond yields in general.

(10) The level and trend of prices of comparable foreign bonds in Wall Street and on other Stock Exchanges.

(11) Effectiveness of exchange control in preventing residents of the countries concerned from acquiring the bonds.

(12) The level of the premium on investment dollars or on similar currencies.

(13) The degree of competition between banks wanting to handle the new issues.

(14) The ability and willingness of issuing houses and under-
     writers to nurse loans that were undersubscribed.

(16) Competition of alternative facilities available to
     borrowers for covering their capital requirements.

The supply of Euro-bonds available for new investment
depends on the volume of new issues and on the willingness of
holders of Euro-bonds to sell their holdings. The flow of new
issues is not even but has its ups and downs, with spells of weeks
and even months during which their totals fall considerably.
Nor is there any regular flow of dealings in earlier issues.
Issuing houses and underwriters usually aim at placing their
portions of the issues privately, and they only take the initiative
for offering them on the secondary market between banks if
there are no ready takers among their clients. Although a high
proportion of the latter acquire the bonds with the intention of
holding them, there is, nevertheless, a fair volume of turnover.
The prices at which bonds change hands in the secondary
market convey some idea about the trend of international
long-term interest rates and influence the terms of new bond
issues.

The popularity of Euro-bonds among investors depends
partly on general considerations such as the interest investors
take in acquiring bonds in general and foreign bonds in particular, confidence in the dollar – in respect of D. mark bonds,
the view taken of revaluation prospects – local and international
political considerations in lending countries and in borrowing
countries, etc. But it is also affected by the availability of, and
yield on, alternative investment facilities. Foreign bonds
quoted in Wall Street have the advantage of a broader market
in the absence of the Interest Equalisation Tax, though Euro-
bonds offer a higher yield. Any change in differentials against
alternative investments is liable to affect the demand for
Euro-bonds.

That demand is also affected by the level of local long-term
rates in countries where they are issued. The extent of this
influence depends largely on the extent to which local residents
are permitted to subscribe. We saw earlier that in Germany

and Switzerland there is no restriction on acquiring such bonds, and even in Holland and Belgium investors are in a position to do so with the aid of investment dollars which are at a small premium against the current exchange rate. As far as these countries are concerned, yields of the dollar bonds have to compete against those of comparable domestic bond issues. On the other hand, in countries such as Britain, where exchange control greatly reduces the possibility of subscriptions by residents, as far as these residents are concerned the bonds have only to compete against yields of foreign bonds which local residents are entitled to replace by the new bonds.

When the bonds are placed outside the countries in which they are issued then the interest rates in the countries where the issues are made matter naturally less than the interest rates in countries whose residents acquire the bonds. Even so, these bonds may be regarded by non-residents as alternative investments to the local bonds of countries in which they are issued. For instance, a Continental investor may acquire Euro-bonds issued in London as an alternative to buying sterling bonds, domestic or foreign, with the aid of external sterling. But considerations of confidence in sterling are liable to prevail.

We saw in the last chapter that, to a large extent, the Euro-bonds are acquired by residents of the borrowing countries themselves if they have full confidence in the solvency of the borrower but wish to hold foreign securities because they may not altogether trust the stability of the local currency, or because they assume that Euro-bonds have a better market. When the bonds are acquired as a hedge against a devaluation of the local currency the yield is a secondary consideration. The attraction of being able to rely on a good bond market may induce investors to accept a slightly lower yield for the sake of the prospects of obtaining a better price when realising the bonds.

Interest rates in the issuing countries determine the cost of the temporary financing of the issues until the bonds are placed with investors. On the assumption that this can be completed in a matter of days or weeks, interest charges for such a brief period should not materially affect the terms on which issuing houses and underwriters are prepared to handle the issue. But if they envisage the possibility of having to nurse a large part of the issue for months they have to consider the costs when negotiating the terms. Indeed the high cost of the temporary financing of the issues might even induce many banks to decline participating in the transaction.

The cost of short-term financing of the transactions with the aid of borrowed Euro-currencies depends partly on the cost of covering the exchange risk. Unless it is deemed safe to leave that risk uncovered, forward rates are to some extent liable to influence the cost of short-term financing of the issues and the terms on which issuing houses and underwriters are willing to participate.

Apart altogether from the level of local short-term interest rates affecting the cost of financing the transactions, conditions of liquidity in the capital markets concerned are also liable to affect interest rates on bonds. Local conditions of liquidity as well as the cost of short-term financing are apt to influence issuing houses and underwriters in their decision whether to assume commitments, even in currencies other than their own.

Since there is no means of knowing how much of the participations in the issue have to be carried and for how long they have to be carried, financing is usually effected with the aid of money at call or at very short notice. That being so, the prospects of tighter conditions in the near future carry the possibilitiy of having to renew these loans at a higher cost.

The volume of funds available for investing in Euro-bonds is apt to chage. Since these bonds are not everybody's cup of tea, the appearance of a number of issues in close succession might congest the market. We saw in the last chapter that the absorbing capacity of the market is liable to become reduced through various circumstances. When that happens, issuing houses and underwriters prefer to forgo the deal unless the terms are made attractive enough to induce the type of investor to whom these bonds appeal to realise other holdings of similar bonds for the sake of investing in the new issues and to induce new sets of investors to take an interest in them. Otherwise issuing houses might deem it necessary to wait with the next issue until funds available for the purpose have been accumulated by the existing limited range of investors who can be relied upon for being interested in them. Self-respecting borrowers may be reluctant to pay higher long-term interest rates, for fear of the effect of such terms on their prestige. For this reason, among others, long-term interest rates on high-class bonds are less flexible than international short-term interest rates.

An all-important consideration affecting interest rates is the view taken on the currency of the bonds. This point is discussed in greater detail in Chapter 16. When there appears to be a possibility of its devaluation it effectively deters a high proportion of potential investors, while others are only interested if the high yield compensates them for the assumption of the additional risk. With the return of confidence in the dollar during 1963–64 and again in 1968 the bonds became distinctly more attractive than they were during dollar scares, though this trend became reversed in 1969 because of the rising trend of interest rates.

The possibility, however remote, of a revaluation in Germany is largely responsible for the increase in the popularity of D. mark bonds among investors. And the possibility of an all-round devaluation, or of a series of devaluations, is the principal *raison d'être* for the demand for bonds issued in terms of composite units of account.

Euro-bonds are apt to be used extensively as a hedge against a devaluation of the investors' own currencies. For this reason the views taken by residents in the countries concerned about the prospects of their own currencies are liable to influence demand for these bonds. Revaluation prospects of the investors' own currencies are also an important factor. Residents in Switzerland or Germany are reluctant to acquire long-term dollar bonds of any kind unless the interest differential compared with bonds in Swiss francs or D. marks is deemed to be sufficiently wide to compensate them for the remote risk of a revaluation of their currency. On the other hand, residents in countries with devaluation-prone currencies might be inclined to hedge against the devaluation of their currencies by acquiring Euro-bonds even at a relatively low yield – provided that they can do so under their exchange regulations or that they can evade those regulations.

Borrowers on their part are not likely to concede a higher yield for the sake of the prospects of a devaluation of the dollar, for it seems highly probable that if ever such a devaluation should be decided upon it would be part of a co-ordinated all-round devaluation to be arranged under the auspices of the International Monetary Fund. Should that be the case, their own relatively soft currencies would be devalued simultaneously with the dollar and probably to at least the same extent. In the unlikely event of an independent devaluation of the dollar, all softer currencies, including those of the borrowing countries, would be certain to follow its example immediately, so that borrowers would not stand to gain in terms of their own currencies.

Euro-dollar rates and other Euro-currency deposit rates affect interest rates on bonds in two senses. They influence the cost of temporary financing of the transactions by issuing houses and underwriters who may employ borrowed Euro-dollars or other Euro-currencies for that purpose. We saw above that if the cost of short-term facilities is high it tends to discourage the issuing houses and underwriters from engaging in such transactions unless the terms of the loan and of the underwriting commission are such as to compensate them for the additional cost, and to enable them to unload their shares without risk of loss or delay.

The other way in which Euro-dollar rates are liable to affect bond interest rates arises from the lengthening tendency of the maturities of Euro-dollar deposits. At the time of writing it is possible to borrow Euro-dollars almost as a matter of routine up to three years, and negotiated transactions are known to have been arranged even up to five years. Conceivably some investors compare the yields of dollar bonds with those of long-term Euro-dollar deposits. Their decision whether to change into or out of bonds must depend on the differentials. As already pointed out, this need not necessarily mean that a bond issue with an average maturity of fifteen years must offer much higher yields than a five-year deposit. If holders of Euro-currency deposits take the view that interest rates are likely to decline, so that they might not be able to renew their deposits on such favourable terms, they might be willing to accept even a lower yield on Euro-bonds than on Euro-currency deposits, since it is assured for a longer period. Moreover, they may feel safe in investing in long-term bonds on the assumption that, should they require their money before the bonds mature they could always realise their investment at a profit, because of the rise in bond prices that would result from lower interest rates.

The views taken by investors on prospects of long-term interest rates, and of the market in fixed interest bearing securities in general, are an important influence which affects equally the attractions of Euro-bonds and of foreign dollar bonds quoted in Wall Street. But any change in the level and trend of foreign bond prices in the United States might in given circumstances affect the Euro-bonds independently of the general view taken of prospects of interest rates, because, as we saw above, these bonds compete, at any rate to a limited extent, with Euro-bonds.

Part of the demand for Euro-bonds is by residents in countries with exchange controls who succeeded in circumventing those controls. To a by no means negligible extent, therefore, the prices of the bonds and their yields are liable to be influenced by changes and prospects of changes in exchange regulations, and even more by changes in the actual or anticipated effectiveness of their application.

As far as the United Kingdom is concerned an additional factor is the level of the premium on investment dollars. At the time of writing that premium practically rules out any demand for straight bonds by U.K. residents, unless they have foreign securities which they wish to replace by such bonds, or possess investment dollars derived from the realisation of such securities. The premium on investment dollars would have to decline very considerably before its fluctuations became a factor affecting the terms of the new issues of Euro-bonds in existing circumstances. With the premium around 50 per cent at the time of writing, this contingency may appear very remote. But it is well to remember that a few years earlier the premium was quite negligible, and that the corresponding premium is kept down now in other financial centres, so that the possibility of its decline to a sufficiently low level to make its use for purchases of Euro-bonds a practical possibility cannot be ruled out.

The extent of competition between rival issuing houses in various financial centres is liable to affect bonds to some degree. We have already recalled that during the 'twenties Central European and other borrowers were able to obtain unduly favourable terms because of the cut-throat competition between American and other issuing houses. Up to the time of writing there has been very little indication of a return to those conditions – presumably because there are so many would-be borrowers that there is enough business to keep all issuing houses busy – but there is enough competition to preclude the possibility of forcing unduly harsh terms on eager borrowers.

Finally, the existence of alternative facilities for covering requirements of long-term capital is also liable to affect the terms of Euro-bond issues. More will be said about this in Chapter 10.

All these effects may be distinct from, and additional to, the various direct effects of Euro-issues, produced through the resulting operations in foreign exchanges, in Euro-currencies, and in the local money markets.

The present chapter does not deal with the specific influence on international interest rates of increased American borrowing and of increased German lending in the Euro-bond market, nor with the specific effect of convertible bond issues on a large scale. These aspects of the subject are dealt with in the chapters related to them.

CHAPTER NINE

Impact on Euro-Dollars

THERE is a degree of similarity in some respects between Euro-bonds and Euro-dollars. Like Euro-dollars, these bonds constitute claims in U.S. dollars, which are actually payable in ordinary U.S. dollars in the United States, even if during the interval between borrowing and repayment the claims involved may change hands any number of times between non-resident holders outside the United States. They represent dollar loans lent largely, though not exclusively, by non-resident holders of dollars. Their markets are mostly in Europe. Their special European character may be ended should they ever be sold to a U.S. resident, just as the European character of a Euro-dollar deposit may be terminated if it is used for payments to residents in the United States, or if its owner ceases to re-deposit it outside the United States.

There are, however, some important differences, apart altogether from the obvious one between long-term bonds and short- or medium-term deposits. When Euro-dollar deposits change hands their nominal amount is unchanged and it is only the deposit rates that are subject to the operation of the market mechanism. On the other hand, interest rates of European dollar bonds remain unchanged, but the prices at which they change hands is subject to market influences. While in the case of Euro-dollars the ultimate debtor is invariably one of the American banks with which the dollars are held on deposit, in the case of European dollar bonds the ultimate debtor is a non-resident, even if payment is to be made by the debtor in U.S. dollars, payable in the United States. Possibly payment may be made in another currency if the investor has an option to demand interest and principal in another currency.

Problem of EDM

There may of course be a substantial difference between the security of the two claims. Euro-dollar deposits are, in spite of their name, short- or medium-term credits and they are entirely unsecured. European dollar bonds, on the other hand, may or may not be secured by specific guarantees, or they may represent a definite charge on tangible assets or specific revenues. In each case there is only a single debtor whose insolvency would affect the investor, while Euro-dollar deposits may have gone through the hands of a succession of borrowers, and default by any one of them is liable to produce chain-reactions that might result in the non-payment of the debt, if a solvent debtor should be prevented by exchange restriction from securing the dollars to replace the amount he failed to receive from his defaulting debtor.

The impact of European dollar bond issues on Euro-dollar rates depends partly on the extent to which the transactions are financed by means of borrowed Euro-dollars or by means of investing Euro-dollars for that purpose by their owners, and partly on the extent to which this form of borrowing takes the place of borrowing Euro-dollar deposits. Euro-dollar rates are also liable to be influenced by the issue terms of, and subsequent yield on, Euro-bonds. Finally, they are liable to be affected indirectly by the effects of such bonds – both through the impact of their issue and through their interest rate – on the dollar rate and on local interest rates.

Euro-bonds are financed by investors to some extent with the aid of long-term Euro-dollar deposits borrowed for that purpose and renewed again and again. In Britain the authorities encourage such use of Euro-dollars by granting licences for borrowing them for periods up to twelve months for financing the acquisition of approved dollar investments. Even so, such transactions must surely be exceptional. The purpose for which borrowed Euro-dollars are used on a large scale is for the temporary financing of the transaction by issuing houses and underwriters, pending the definite placing of the bonds with investors. Euro-dollars, or for that matter any other Euro-currencies, are eminently suitable for that purpose, since issuing

houses and banks of high standing that participate in underwriting can very easily borrow large amounts at a very short
notice at rates that often compare favourably with the cost of
alternative forms of borrowing. In given circumstances interest
is saved by borrowing very short-term Euro-dollars and
repeatedly renewing the deposits if by their maturity the bonds
have not been disposed of.

Euro-bond issues are usually accompanied by a demand for
Euro-dollars for such temporary financing and, perhaps to
some extent, for permanent financing by investors. This
temporary demand, if on a sufficiently large scale, is liable to
affect Euro-dollar rates. The repayment of such credits after
the bonds have been placed with investors reverses this effect.
If, however, a series of bond issue transactions follow each
other in close succession the effect of the repayment is offset
by that of new temporary borrowing.

The institutional change of the development of the market
in Euro-bonds has resulted in a once-for-all increase in the
demand for Euro-dollar credits, in that a certain amount
of Euro-dollars are used more or less all the time for such temporary financing even if they are repaid and re-borrowed over
and over again. Any increase in the volume of Euro-bond
issues, or in the delays of placing the newly issued bonds with
investors, tends to cause an increase in the Euro-dollar requirements for that purpose and tends to raise Euro-dollar rates.
Any decline in the volume of bond issues or a shortening of
delays for unloading the bonds tends to cause a decline in the
requirements of Euro-dollars for that purpose and a decline in
Euro-dollar rates.

Euro-dollars are not borrowed systematically on a large scale
for the purpose of a permanent financing of Euro-bond holdings. In normal conditions the interest differential between
three years Euro-dollar deposits and even relatively short-term
ten to fifteen year dollar bonds is too narrow to make it worth
while for investors to finance permanently holdings of such
bonds by such means. He would expose himself to the risk of
having to renew the Euro-dollars at a much higher rate.

Unless he holds very strong views about the likelihood of a decline in Euro-dollar rates he is not likely to take such a risk. The lower Euro-dollar rates are the higher is the risk that renewal might have to be affected at much less favourable rates. Moreover, there is also a remote risk that, over a period of years, something might develop that would interfere with the functioning of the Euro-dollar market – such as the adoption of new exchange restrictions – so that renewal of deposits could no longer be effected as a matter of routine. Such a change might force holders to resort to some costlier method of financing or to sell their investment – possibly at an inopportune moment.

It is of course conceivable that a decline in Euro-dollar rates, or a rise in interest rates on Euro-bonds, or a combination of both, might widen the differential to a level at which it would appear worth while to take the risk attached to financing the bonds with the aid of borrowed Euro-dollars. On the other hand, on the basis of actual experience in 1969 it is evidently possible for Euro-dollar rates to rise considerably above Euro-bond rates over relatively long periods.

Interest rates on new Euro-bond issues are liable to affect Euro-dollar rates by influencing borrowers' decisions whether or not to resort to bond issues in preference to covering their requirements with the aid of Euro-dollar credits. It also influences investors' decision whether to tie down their capital in long-term dollar bonds or hold Euro-dollar deposits on the assumption that Euro-dollar rates are more likely to rise than to decline.

While borrowers' decisions, once made, cannot be changed until they want to raise additional funds or re-finance maturing debts, investors are in a position to reach new decisions at any time. Should they decide that the differential between Euro-dollar rates and yields on existing Euro-bonds make it worth their while to replace their Euro-dollar deposits by such bonds the resulting operations tend to lower yields on bonds and to raise Euro-dollar rates. Conversely, should they take the opposite view, the resulting operations tend to raise yields on bonds and to lower Euro-dollar rates.

The following is a summary of the ways in which issue of Euro-bonds tend to cause a rise in Euro-dollar rates:

(1) The transactions may involve additional temporary financing with the aid of borrowed Euro-dollars whenever there is an excess of new temporary requirements for that purpose over repayments of deposits previously borrowed for that purpose.

(2) Wide differentials make it appear immediately profitable to risk permanent financing of Euro-bond holdings with the aid of long-term Euro-dollar deposits to be renewed on maturity

(3) During periods when Euro-dollar rates are abnormally high it may appear profitable in the long run to risk a permanent financing of Euro-bond holdings with short-term Euro-dollars on the assumption that Euro-dollar rates are likely to fall.

The ways in which Euro-bond operations tend to cause a decline in Euro-dollar rates may be summarised as follows:

(1) Borrowed Euro-dollar deposits may be repaid out of the proceeds of Euro-bond issues.

(2) Borrowing by means of such issues may be resorted to in preference to borrowing Euro-dollars.

(3) In so far as diversion of foreign long-term borrowing from New York causes New York interest rates to decline, to some extent Euro-dollar rates tends to move in sympathy.

(4) A decline in the yield of Euro-bonds tends to cause a decline in Euro-dollar rates also by discouraging the borrowing of Euro-dollars for the purpose financing the issue or the holding of such bonds.

(5) An appreciation of forward dollars resulting from the beneficial effect of Euro-bond issues on the dollar increases the cost of borrowing Euro-dollar deposits for the purpose of swapping the proceeds into other currencies. It would reduce therefore the demand for Euro-dollars.

It is impossible to assess even approximately the relative extent to which the two sets of conflicting influences are liable

D

to affect Euro-dollar rates on balance. All we can do is to indicate their effects in either direction and hope that later, in possession of more experience in the working of the system, it might become possible to arrive at more definite and more helpful conclusions. As a tentative conclusion I am inclined to believe that, on balance, the Euro-bond issues, in so far as they are additional to the amount that would be issued in New York in the absence of facilities in Europe, and in so far as they constitute an alternative to borrowing of Euro-dollars tends to cause a fall in Euro-dollar rates, unless such issues are financed with the aid of Euro-dollars on a very large scale.

To what extent is the effect on Euro-dollar rates, whatever it may be, due to the choice of the dollar as the currency in which the bonds are issued? Does it modify the effect of the device on Euro-dollar rates to the extent to which the Euro-bond issues do not assume the form of dollar bonds?

In so far as the effect is due to the use of the new facilities as alternatives to short- and medium-term investment in Euro-dollar deposits, possibly there would be less inducement for making the change if the bonds were in terms of some other monetary unit. Their yield is not so easily comparable with that of Euro-dollar deposits. Those wishing to remain in dollars would not be interested. Most of those inclined to switch into some other currencies would probably be influenced by considerations other than yield. If the foreign bonds issued in Europe are issued in a currency that is widely expected to be revalued – such as the D. mark at the time of writing – many investors might be inclined to accept even a lower yield than the yield on Euro-dollar deposits, for the sake of the prospects of a capital profit on revaluation. The same is true, of course, in respect of bonds convertible into equities which are acquired for their prospects of capital appreciation. Safeguards against devaluation provided by the formula of the composite unit of account, and the renunciation of revaluation profit that its adoption implies, introduces yet another set of considerations influencing investors' decisions when comparing the yield of Euro-bonds with that of Euro-dollar deposits.

The extent to which Euro-dollars are used for the temporary financing of bond issues is liable to be affected by the cost of forward covering if the bonds are in a different currency. On the other hand, the use of borrowed Euro-dollars for permanent financing of holdings of Euro-bonds would not be affected, because investors would not be likely to cover the forward exchange, except on bonds due to be repaid shortly.

The use of a non-dollar currency unit for the denomination of the bonds reduces the extent to which the proceeds are used for repayment of Euro-dollar deposits, if the borrower envisages a devaluation of the dollar. Likewise a diversion of borrowing from the Euro-dollar market to the Euro-bond market would be effected by the choice of Euro-bonds of a different denomination owing to the possibility of a devaluation or a revaluation of the currency concerned.

The effect of the diversion of foreign borrowing from the United States on the American balance of payments and, through that effect, on Euro-dollar rates, is the same whether Euro-bonds are in terms of dollars or of other currency units. The same is true about the effect of Euro-bond issues on foreign demand for American credit facilities.

To the extent to which the effect of Euro-bond issues is favourable to the American balance of payments and, through it, to the dollar, it tends to reduce Euro-dollar rates in the following ways:

(1) By inspiring confidence in the dollar, thereby reducing demand for Euro-dollars by speculators for the purpose of selling the proceeds in order to create a short position.

(2) By strengthening the spot dollar, thereby obviating the necessity for dear money measures in the United States in its defence. Since the Euro-dollar market always tries to keep its borrowing rates just above deposit rates in the United States, this tends to cause a decline in Euro-dollar rates, or at any rate it prevents an increase that would occur otherwise.

We saw above that, in so far as an increase of confidence in the dollar through the effect of Euro-bond issues tends to cause an appreciation of forward dollars it tends to reduce demand for Euro-dollar credits, because of the increase in the cost of covering the exchange risk on deposits switched into some other currency for the duration of the loan. Since borrowers have to give away more in the form of forward dollar premium, they can only afford to pay lower Euro-dollar rates.

On the other hand, in so far as the new practice results in a reduction in the volume of Euro-dollar deposits through their consolidation into long-term indebtedness, it causes a rise in Euro-dollar rates in face of persistent unchanged demand.

Owing to the importance of this aspect of the new problems, it is necessary to examine with great care the impact of dollar bond issues on the volume of Euro-dollar deposits. On the face of it, the issue of Euro-bonds must tend to reduce the turnover in the Euro-dollar market, because some deposits are immobilised through their use for financing bond holdings, and many of them are repaid out of the proceeds of the loans. On that ground it would appear that dollar bond issues consolidate some of the floating funds represented by Euro-dollar deposits. After all, individual borrowers do consolidate their floating debt and individual lenders of deposits do transform their short-term investments into long-term investments. Obvious as such conclusions may seem at first sight, for that very reason they call for closer examination.

A reduction in the volume of borrowed Euro-dollars, whether through consolidation or repayment, need not be more than purely temporary, so long as there is no reduction in the overall demand for Euro-dollars. For in the Euro-dollar market, as indeed in all good markets, a two-way 'Say's Law' is in operation – supply creates its demand, but likewise demand creates its supply. If short-term investments and floating debts are consolidated simultaneously and to the same extent as the reduction of demand for Euro-dollars, the turnover would decline. But if additional demand should develop, the would-be borrowers can satisfy their requirements if necessary at the cost of bidding up the rates. A rise in rates tends to attract additional dormant dollars to the Euro-dollar market.

Conversely, if repayment of Euro-bonds is unaccompanied by a corresponding increase in the demand for Euro-dollars, a decline in Euro-dollar rates caused by the 'de-funding' of Euro-bonds, tends to stimulate additional demand.

Practical experience gained in a number of instances confirms the view that demand for Euro-dollars tends to cause an increase of its depleted supply. During 1963 there was a sharp reduction in the amount of dollars Central Banks had lent directly or indirectly to the Euro-dollar market. In spite of that there was no decline in the turnover – indeed it continued to expand – because the effect of the withdrawals on Euro-dollar rates induced other holders of dollar deposits, both American and non-American, to lend their deposits in the Euro-dollar market. It seems that, given the pressure of the demand for Euro-dollar deposits, rates tend to become adapted to a level at which additional supply is attracted to replace supplies withdrawn from the market. If certain lenders or classes of lenders, such as investors in Euro-bonds, reduce their lendings of Euro-dollars, other owners of dollars take their place as a result of a rise in Euro-dollar rates.

In any case, we saw above that temporary financing of bond issues tends in given circumstances to raise Euro-dollar rates. To the extent to which this occurs additional supplies may be attracted to the market, so that in spite of the consolidation of some deposits the net result of the operation might well be an actual increase in the total volume of Euro-dollar deposits.

The basic fact of the situation is that, owing to the elasticity of Euro-dollar supplies and the inadequacy of other supplies of credit, potential demand for Euro-dollar deposits is virtually unlimited. Any fall in the rate tends to cause an increase in demand by creditworthy borrowers, which again tends to restore the rate to its original level.

Euro-bond issues may be financed not only with Euro-dollar deposits but also with any other Euro-currency deposits. Although it is simpler for subscribers to use Euro-dollars he already holds, and for banks to borrow Euro-dollars for financing the issue, they might find it more advantageous to use some other Euro-currencies. Borrowers of such currencies might sell them outright, or they might want to cover the exchange risk by swapping into dollars. Likewise, holders of Euro-currency deposits either sell their currencies against dollars or cover the exchange risk at the same time. Since forward rates tend to adjust themselves to interest parities between Euro-currencies there is usually very little advantage or disadvantage in choosing one Euro-currency in preference to another, though occasionally discrepancies which would influence their choice might arise. Or subscribers may hold deposits in one of the Euro-currencies other than Euro-dollar. Advantages from using other Euro-currencies are more pronounced when, owing to the pre-vailing level or prospects of the spot rates, it is not deemed necessary to cover the exchange risk when borrowing such Euro-currencies. To the extent to which Euro-currencies other than Euro-dollars are used it is of course their rates that tends to be affected by the transactions.

Conversely, Euro-dollar rates and the turnover in Euro-dollars are liable to be affected by the issue of bonds other than Euro-bonds, in so far as the transactions are financed with the aid of Euro-dollars. There is indeed no reason why issuing houses should not use Euro-dollars for financing bonds issued in terms of composite units of account or in terms of any hard currency or in terms of their local currency. Nor, for that matter, is there any particular reason why such temporary financing should not be effected in cases of domestic capital transactions of every kind. The Euro-dollar market provides very convenient facilities for such temporary financing, and Euro-dollar rates are liable to be influenced by them, regardless of whether the capital issues consist of domestic or foreign bonds or equities. This has to be borne in mind in order to avoid a misconception that the influence of Euro-bond issues on Euro-dollars is necessarily a special case, even though it has some special aspects.

The main difference between the impact of dollar bond issues and that of capital issues in general on Euro-dollars lies in the fact that in the case of the former there is some possibility of time arbitrage, in spite of the fact that, apart altogether from differences in the length of maturity, the two investments are far from being absolutely interchangeable.

Now that an active market has developed in Euro-bonds, speculative transactions in such bonds are apt to be financed with the aid of Euro-dollars on an extensive scale. Should such operations assume considerable dimensions – as they might well assume as a result of the spectacular increase in the outstanding amount of Euro-bonds – the ups and downs of speculative activity in the Euro-bond market might well affect Euro-dollar rates in the same way as the ups and downs of speculative activities in gold, exchanges or foreign equities affect them from time to time.

Although the effect of non-dollar Euro-bonds on Euro-dollars was touched upon repeatedly in this chapter, we propose to return to this subject in Chapter 12 dealing with D. mark bond issues.

CHAPTER TEN

Impact on the Dollar Exchange

THE main object of the Interest Equalisation Tax, to relieve the American balance of payments of pressure due to the excessive foreign long-term borrowing in New York, was served by the new tax partly through discouraging U.S. residents from subscribing to such loans and partly through giving European financial centres a chance to develop their capital markets for absorbing domestic and foreign capital issues which would otherwise be floated in New York. The latter object was also intended to be served by the issue of the excellent report published by the United States Treasury early in 1964, referred to in Chapter 1, providing a wealth of valuable information about the facilities, practices and comparative advantages and defects of Western European capital markets.

In taking these steps to develop capital issuing activities in Europe the U.S. authorities were doubtless aware that the resulting additional activities would assume mainly the form of foreign dollar bond issues. No doubt they had hoped that facilities would also develop for European domestic issues in domestic currencies to cover domestic requirements, especially by France and other countries where industries and others in need of capital found it easier and cheaper to borrow in New York than in their own inadequately developed domestic capital markets.

The figures relating to foreign issues in New York prior to the change of policy give an exaggerated idea of the actual burden of long-term lending abroad on the American balance of payments. Already before the war, and again since the war, a substantial proportion of European dollar loans issued in New York was actually placed in Europe either immediately at the time of their issue or through subsequent placings and purchases. Estimates of that proportion for recent years vary between one-quarter and three-quarters of the total. Even so, the burden represented by the net amount of foreign loans absorbed by the United States must have been substantial, additional as it was to heavy U.S. Government spendings abroad.

The extent to which an expansion of European capital markets relieves pressure on the dollar depends also on the extent to which borrowers use American long-term bank credits as an alternative to making public issues in New York. This is known to have been done after the adoption of the Interest Equalisation Tax to a by no means negligible extent. To meet requirements of foreign borrowers prevented by the tax from issuing loans in New York, American banks were prepared to grant credits for much longer periods than had been customary.

The Euro-dollar market, too, provided foreign long-term borrowers with facilities which were to some extent an alternative to those provided by the New York bond issue market. Maximum maturities of Euro-dollar deposits became much longer after the adoption of the Interest Equalisation Tax. The London market in Certificates of Deposits provides since 1967 facilities which replace to some extent the capital resources provided by New York until 1964. In so far as such funds had already been lent outside the United States their re-lending for longer periods does not impose any direct additional burden on the American balance of payments. In so far as such lendings replace the issue of bonds that would have been made in New York, and to the extent to which such bonds would have been actually retained in the United States, it appears on the face of it that a diversion of foreign borrowing from the New York capital market to the Euro-dollar market tends to bring relief to the dollar, at any rate in a negative sense.

The next question is in what sense and to what extent the choice of the dollar as the currency in terms of which the Euro-bonds are issued stands to affect the dollar. The answer depends on the nature of dollar holdings raised by the lender

D 2

and the purpose for which the borrower makes use of them. Dollars provided by issuing houses, underwriters and investors may originate in the following ways:

(1) Residents outside the United States buy dollars.
(2) Residents outside the United States employ their dollar deposits or borrow Euro-dollar deposits.
(3) Residents outside the U.S. employ their own dollar deposits or the proceeds of other realised dollar assets.
(4) U.S. residents invest funds legitimately held abroad.
(5) U.S. residents invest their existing 'refugee' funds.
(6) U.S. residents employ funds specially transferred abroad for that purpose.

Demand for dollars in the foreign exchange market by subscribers, or by issuing houses and underwriters who have to provide the amount not covered by subscribers, obviously supports the dollar exchange. If, however, subscribers are British residents and the demand is for investment dollars it does not affect the dollar exchange, except perhaps indirectly, through the psychological effect of a widening of the premium on investment dollars. If the demand is for the Dutch or Belgian equivalents of investment dollars and the Dutch or Belgian authorities support the rate, the reduction of their dollar reserves tends to strengthen the dollar potentially, without affecting its exchange rate. But if the transaction entails a transfer of foreign holdings of dollars from official reserves into private hands it may constitute a potential threat to the dollar.

The effect on the dollar exchange of the use of Euro-dollars for the purpose of subscribing to Euro-bonds is a most difficult question to answer. It is indeed hard to resist the temptation to call it 'the 64 Euro-dollar question'. We saw in the last chapter that both the temporary financing of the transaction by issuing houses and underwriters with the aid of borrowed Euro-dollars and the permanent financing of such bond holdings by investors with the aid of their Euro-dollar deposits tend to cause a rise in Euro-dollar rates. On the other hand, borrowing by issuing Euro-bonds instead of borrowing

Euro-dollars, or the consolidation of Euro-dollar debts out of the proceeds of the dollar bond issues, tends to cause Euro-dollar rates to decline.

The effect of such movements of Euro-dollar rates on the dollar exchange rate is analysed in detail in my recent book, *The Euro-Dollar System*. The following are the points relevant to our present subject:

(1) An increase of Euro-dollar rates tends to attract additional funds to the Euro-dollar market. This in itself does not necessarily involve foreign exchange transactions, but if it does involve acquisition of dollars through the purchases in the foreign exchange market it affects the dollar favourably.

(2) If additional Euro-dollars are acquired temporarily by means of swap transactions the favourable effect on spot dollars is somewhat mitigated by the unfavourable effect on forward dollars. For a detailed consideration of the effects of swap transactions on forward rates and of spot rates I must refer the reader to my book *A Dynamic Theory of Forward Exchange*.

(3) An increase of Euro-dollar rates tends to affect the forward dollar unfavourably also by changing its interest parities. Forward dollars tend to adjust themselves to their interest parities between Euro-dollar and other Euro-currencies, though in actual practice it is usually the other Euro-currency rates that adjust themselves to forward dollar rates and Euro-dollar rates.

(4) If a rise in Euro-dollar rates leaves the other interest parities of the forward dollar substantially unaffected it tends to cause an undervaluation of the forward dollar in relation to those other parities. This may give rise to outward arbitrage from New York, tending to affect the spot dollar unfavourably.

If the net effect of the European dollar bond issues on Euro-dollar rates is a decline it tends to affect the dollar in the following ways:

(1) It tends to divert dollars from the Euro-dollar market.

If this assumes the form of selling dollars by owners of
Euro-dollar deposits it causes a depreciation.

(2) If the dollars diverted from the Euro-dollar market
are disposed of temporarily by means of swap transactions its unfavourable effect on spot dollars is somewhat mitigated by its favourable effect on forward
dollars.

(3) A decline of Euro-dollar rates tends to affect the forward
dollar favourably also by changing the interest parities
between Euro-currency rates.

(4) If a decline in Euro-dollar rates leaves the other interest
parities of the forward dollar substantially unaffected it
tends to cause an overvaluation of the forward dollar in
relation to those parities. This may give rise to inward
arbitrage to New York, tending to affect the spot dollar
favourably.

In addition to these direct effects, a rise or a decline in
Euro-dollar rates caused by Euro-bond issues is liable to affect
the dollar also indirectly. We saw in the last chapter that the
supply of Euro-dollars, if depleted through their consolidation
into long-term investments, tends to became automatically
replenished if the change causes an increase in Euro-dollar
rates. If the dollars transferred to the Euro-dollar market in
such circumstances are foreign owned, the net result is an
increased average fluidity of the unchanged external floating
indebtedness of the United States. If, on the other hand, the
additional dollars attracted to the Euro-dollar market are
American-owned the net result is an increase in the gross
external floating debt, while leaving the external consolidated
debt unchanged. The result is a weakening in the defences of
the dollar.

Another way in which a rise in Euro-dollar rates caused by
Euro-bond issues is liable to affect the dollar is by inducing
foreign holders of dollars to retain their dollars for the sake of
the higher yields. Although reductions of foreign dollar holdings
may be decided upon for other causes, there must surely be
many borderline cases in which case a rise in the yield would

tip the balance against selling the dollars. To the extent to which such effect is produced the issue of Euro-bonds tends to support the dollar, at any rate in a negative sense.

If the net effect of Euro-bond issues is a decline in Euro-dollar rates which diverts dollars from the Euro-dollar market, in so far as the Euro-dollars concerned were foreign-owned the net result is a reduced fluidity of the external floating debt of the United States. If, on the other hand, withdrawals from the Euro-dollar market are on American account, it reduces the fluid external short-term debt of the United States, at the same time as reducing the external liquid assets.

If a decline in Euro-dollar rates induces foreign holders to sell their dollars because of the inadequacy of their yield, the effect is detrimental to the dollar exchange. In a negative sense, non-residents may decide against acquiring dollars owing to the reduced yield on Euro-dollar deposits.

The investment in Euro-bonds of American funds which are held already abroad – such as reserves of American subsidiaries – does not in itself affect the dollar, except possibly in a negative sense to the extent to which such bonds are acquired in preference to acquiring foreign bonds held in the United States, or to repatriations in any form. Such transactions would involve purchases of dollars that would not occur if Euro-bonds were bought instead.

There is no likelihood of any additional outflow of American capital for the sake of investment in Euro-bonds. United States residents who are tempted to transfer their capital abroad in a way as to be untraceable by the fiscal authorities may or may not decide to do so, but their decision is guided by considerations other than any special attractions of Euro-bonds as investments.

Most effects produced on the dollar through financing of Euro-bond issues with the aid of Euro-dollars are identical with the effects produced by financing D. mark or composite unit of account bond issues, or indeed by financing any domestic issues made abroad. In so far as such issues are not payable in dollars they would of course not result in any demand for dollars in the foreign exchange market that might be caused by the issue of bonds in dollar denomination. But in so far as in the absence of adequate issuing facilities in Europe such issues would have been floated in New York, their diversion to Europe obviously relieves pressure on the dollar.

Hitherto we have been dealing with the effect of financing Euro-bond issues. Our next step is to examine the effect of the use made by borrowers of the proceeds of such issues. They may employ their dollars for the following purposes:

(1) Repayment of outstanding dollar liabilities.
(2) Alternative financing to borrowing dollars in the United States.
(3) Alternative financing to borrowing Euro-dollars.
(4) Payment for imports from the United States.
(5) Payment for imports from other countries.
(6) Conversion into the borrowers' local currency through the sale of the dollars in the foreign exchange market.
(7) Surrender of the dollars to the borrowers' monetary authorities.

If the proceeds are used for repayment of dollar liabilities it leaves the dollar exchange unaffected, except in a negative sense to the extent to which, in the absence of the Euro-bond issues, the debtors would have had to buy dollars in the market in order to meet their liabilities. Repayment of foreign debt, whether through purchases of dollars in the market or through borrowing dollars for long term from holders who are not resident in the United States, tends to strengthen the technical position of the dollar, inasmuch as it reduces the American external floating debt.

We already saw above that the issue of Euro-bonds as an alternative to borrowing dollars in the United States tends in a negative sense, to relieve the dollar of the pressure that would be caused by such borrowing.

If borrowers cover their requirements by means of dollar bond issues instead of by means of borrowing Euro-dollar deposits, in a negative sense it tends to keep down Euro-dollar rates which would have been caused to rise as a result of such borrowing. If Euro-dollar deposits are repaid out of the proceeds of the loans the resulting decline in Euro-dollar rates would affect the dollar in a sense described above when dealing with the effects of the financing of Euro-bonds with the aid of Euro-dollars. The question is whether the sum total of the additional demand for Euro-dollars by issuing houses and underwriters and the reduction of the supply of Euro-dollars through their use by investors for subscribing the bonds is larger or smaller than the total of repayments of Euro-dollar deposits out of the proceeds of the loan and that of the covering of requirements with the aid of dollar bond issues instead of borrowing Euro-dollars. It is the net balance that determines the effect of bond issues on Euro-dollar rates and, through them, on dollar rates.

The use of the proceeds of the Euro-bond issues for payments for American exports which in the absence of such issues would have been paid through dollar purchases tends to affect the dollar unfavourably in a negative sense. But if the operation's earlier phases support the dollar in the ways described above, to that extent the negative adverse effect is cancelled out. If the U.S. exports paid for out of the proceeds of the bond issues are additional to those which would have taken place in the absence of the transactions then the favourable effects of the earlier phases of the operations will not be offset. What matters is to avoid reaching the false conclusion that the favourable effects can duplicate themselves – that Euro-bond issues tend to affect the dollar favourably, first through the acquisition of the dollars by the lenders and then, in addition, through their use in payment to the United States by the borrowers.

The use of the proceeds in payment for exports by other countries does not affect the dollar, unless the purchase of non-American goods is made as an alternative to purchases of American goods which would have taken place in the absence of the transaction. In that case the effect is, of course, unfavourable.

If the conversion of the proceeds of dollar bonds into local currency takes place in the open market the effect on the dollar is unfavourable. There is no such direct effect if the borrowers surrender the proceeds to their Central Banks. In that case the defences of the dollar might be affected favourably as a result of the transfer of foreign-owned dollars from private ownership to ownership by the monetary authorities, always provided that the latter are prepared to accumulate their external reserve in the form of dollars instead of availing themselves of their right to withdraw gold. On that assumption the transfer of dollars into official ownership reduces potential pressure that would arise through subsequent selling of dollars by private holders.

The dollar is affected favourably by the debtors' subsequent purchases of dollars connected with payments of interest and repayments of capital. Secondary effects of the purchases depend, however, on the ways in which interest and principal are spent by their recipients. If the receipt of the dollars obviates the necessity for them to buy dollars which they would have had to buy otherwise, the dollar rate would remain unaffected on balance.

The existence of large holdings of marketable dollar bonds held outside the United States carries the possibility of an aggravation of pressure on the dollar during periods of devaluation scares. Holders of such bonds are not quite as liable to be scared into getting out of dollars as holders of liquid dollar balances, but the difference is merely one of degree. If the buyers of the dollar bonds have to purchase the dollars, this offsets the effect of the sale of their proceeds in the foreign exchange market, but if the buyers already possess the dollars or borrow them while the sellers of the bonds sell the dollars the effect is additional selling pressure on the dollar.

Evidently the effects of Euro-bond issues on the dollar are extremely complex and conflicting. Allowing for the negative effect produced by safeguarding the dollar against pressure due to overlending abroad, it is safe, however, to conclude that the effect is on balance distinctly favourable. The effect of the use of the dollar as the currency in which the loans are issued is also favourable, on balance, to the dollar. Apart from other considerations the fact that the new device has provided the dollar with an additional international use should work in its favour, at any rate in the absence of abnormal circumstances.

Although the effect of European issues of Euro-bonds on the dollar is of outstanding importance, it is necessary to examine also their effects on other exchanges. The effects of such transactions on the exchanges of the borrowing countries are too obvious to call for detailed analysis, and so are the effects on the exchanges of the investing countries. But the effect on the exchanges of entrepôt markets deserve some attention. This subject was already touched upon in Chapter 5.

Sterling liable to be affected by the issue of Euro-bonds in London in the following circumstances (which also apply to other intermediary centres):

(1) If non-resident sterling is converted into dollars in order to subscribe to the new issues.

(2) If non-residents realise their holdings of sterling securities and lend the proceeds against dollars on the Euro-sterling market. Although such transactions only affect the Euro-sterling rate, a rise of that rate might produce an adverse psychological effect on sterling.

(3) If residents subscribe with the aid of investment dollars the resulting widening of the premium on investment dollars would create an unfavourable psychological effect, and it would increase the temptation for U.K. residents to evade the exchange control.

(4) If non-residents subscribe with the aid of borrowed Euro-sterling the resulting increase in Euro-sterling rates would tend to cause a depreciation of forward sterling. The extent of that effect would be, however, purely marginal because, more often than not, Euro-sterling rates adapt themselves to Euro-dollar rates and forward sterling rates rather than influence the latter.

(5) If non-residents subscribe with the aid of borrowed Euro-dollars or if they employ their own Euro-dollars for financing their holdings of dollar bonds the resulting rise in Euro-dollar rates would cause an appreciation of

forward sterling, in so far as Euro-sterling rates do not adapt themselves to the changes in Euro-dollar rates.

(6) The direct and indirect effect of the Euro-bond trans-action on British invisible exports tends to benefit sterling to a minor degree.

(7) Any favourable effect of the transactions on the dollar is liable to be at the expense of sterling to some extent, even if the funds are provided by foreign investors out of resources other than non-resident sterling accounts or borrowed Euro-sterling.

On balance the adverse effect on sterling, if any, is likely to be moderate, and in given circumstances the effect might even be favourable. If currencies other than the dollar are employed the effect is marginally more likely to be favourable, or is likely to be marginally less unfavourable.

CHAPTER ELEVEN

Impact on Domestic *for* Interest Rates

WE saw in Chapter 6 how domestic interest rates in the United
States, in countries where Euro-bonds are issued, in countries
which acquired these bonds, and in borrowing countries are
liable to affect the long-term interest rates represented by the
terms of issue of Euro-bonds and by their subsequent yields.
The effect is, however, reciprocal. The present chapter is to
examine how such international long-term interest rates are
liable to affect domestic interest rates in the United States
and in other countries concerned.

First of all, we must inquire into the ways in which issues of
Euro-bonds tend to affect the domestic interest structure in
New York. The basic fact of the situation is that the American
bond market is immensely wide. Because of this, in spite of any
conceivable increase in the issuing activity of dollar bonds in
Europe, it is unlikely to amount to more than a modest fraction
of the issuing activity of domestic bonds in the United States.
The extent to which European issues could conceivably compete
for the immense volume of American long-term capital invested
or available for investment in bonds would be negligible even in
the absence of the Interest Equalisation Tax. For this reason it
would appear that any direct influence of interest rates or yields
on Euro-bonds on interest rates or yields of dollar bonds in
general in the United States must always be purely marginal.
The tip of the tail is not likely to move the dog to any perceptible
extent.

The one section of the American bond market in which there
is a possibility of a noteworthy direct effect is the market for
foreign dollar bonds. Although such bonds are quoted in Wall
Street, their main market is over the counter. Euro-bonds

compete with these bonds, at any rate to the relatively moderate extent to which residents in the United States are in a position to invest in Euro-bonds without coming under the provisions of the Interest Equalisation Tax. European dollar bonds issued before the announcement of that tax are not subject to that tax and would offer, therefore, advantages as an alternative investment for American residents should their yields decline below those of corresponding New York issues.

There are, however, indirect ways in which actual issues of dollar bonds in Europe, rather than their terms of issue or the subsequent yield on those issues, is liable to affect domestic interest rates in the United States.

(1) They relieve pressure on the dollar. We saw in Chapter 9 that, although the impact of Euro-bond issues on the dollar exchange rate is highly involved and obscure, it stands to reason that on balance the diversion of foreign borrowing from New York does tend to benefit the dollar exchange. To the extent to which it does, it obviates the need for defending the dollar by means of high interest rates or other disinflationary measures leading to a rise of domestic interest rates in the United States. In this respect non-dollar Euro-bond issues tend to produce the same effect as dollar issues. What matters is that foreign long-term borrowing is diverted from New York and that Americans can borrow in Europe.

(2) To the extent to which lending abroad would result in a drain on the gold reserve and would reduce domestic liquidity the diversion of foreign capital issues from New York and American borrowing abroad create more plentiful credit and capital resources within the United States – not only in a negative sense. But in view of the immense capital resources and requirements of the United States, the difference is not likely to be very large.

(3) We already discussed in great detail in Chapter 9 how the issues of Euro-bonds tend to influence Euro-dollar rates. The latter in turn exert some degree of influence on the

domestic interest rate structure in the United States. This is a highly involved subject and for its details I must refer the reader to my book *The Euro-Dollar System: Practice and Theory of International Interest Rates*, Revised Edition, Chapter 11, which shows that Euro-dollar rates affect American domestic interest rates in the following ways:

(*a*) Through competition of Euro-dollar facilities with American short-term dollar investment or borrowing facilities.

(*b*) Through providing additional facilities for inward or outward interest arbitrage.

(*c*) Through providing additional or alternative facilities for speculation against the dollar.

(*d*) Through influencing official monetary policies.

These effects are highly involved and obscure and to a large extent they are liable to cancel each other out. Whether the net effect of issuing Euro-bonds is a rise or fall in Euro-dollar rates, it tends to react on American domestic short-term interest rates. A rise in Euro-dollar rates is particularly liable to affect the American domestic interest rates structure if American banks are large-scale borrowers in the Euro-dollar market, as they were in 1968–69, or if they want to outbid Euro-dollar rates in so far as they can do so under Regulation Q. Rates in the market for Certificates of Deposits are also a factor. Rates in the market for Federal Funds on the eve of weekends and of holidays decline as a result of the use of Euro-dollars for short-term arbitrage.

It is probably in respect of the market in Certificates of Deposits that the extensive use of Euro-bond issues for repayment of Euro-dollar deposits or for avoiding the borrowing of such deposits can neutralise, and more than neutralise, the effect of using Euro-dollars for temporary or permanent financing of the bond issues.

(4) The expansion in the volume of convertible bond issues by American corporations in Europe might conceivably

attain a stage at which it could affect interest rates and convertibility premiums of domestic issues of such bonds Already in 1968 the terms obtainable in Europe began to compete with the terms obtainable in the domestic market.

(5) Euro-bond issues affect interest rates abroad. We shall try to examine below how and to what extent Euro-bond issues are liable to affect domestic interest rates in the issuing countries, in the investing countries and in the borrowing countries. In given circumstances changes in interest rates in these countries may affect American domestic interest rates, especially short-term interest rates. The pressure repeatedly exerted by the United States Government on European Governments to abstain from Bank rate increases in order to be able to keep down interest rates in the United States shows how sensitive the American interest rate structure is to changes in European interest rates.

The next step is to investigate the effects on domestic interest rates in countries whose banks participate in issues of Euro-bonds but whose residents are prevented by exchange control from acquiring such issues except with the aid of investment currencies. The effects on domestic interest rates in the United Kingdom of Eurobond issues made in London are produced in the following ways:

(1) Through sales of non-resident sterling balances against dollars bought for subscribing to such issues. If the resulting weakness of sterling necessitates an increase in the extent of official support of sterling it might contribute towards inducing the authorities to defend sterling by means of higher interest rates.

(2) Through diverting non-resident sterling from loans to the London money market, to local authorities, to hire-purchase finance houses, etc., and from investment in sterling bills. If large amounts of non-resident sterling are used by subscribers to Euro-dollar bonds the reduction in the supply of such foreign funds available

for the above purposes might affect British domestic interest rates on a broad front. The most obvious instance is the effect produced on Treasury bill rates by a decline in the amount of tenders on foreign account, that would be brought about by a diversion of foreign funds on a large scale into the market of new foreign dollar bond issues.

(3) Through its effect on Euro-dollar rates. This should tend to affect forward sterling rates – though, as we saw in the last chapter, that effect is purely marginal – and through them short-term interest rates in London.

(4) Through its effect on Euro-sterling rates which would rise if much Euro-sterling is invested in Euro-bonds and if owners of external account sterling do not wish to employ their funds in the Euro-sterling market.

(5) Through its effect on inter-bank sterling rates, if the financing of the transactions involves much direct borrowing between London banks.

(6) Through its effect on domestic interest rates in the United States, in investing countries and in borrowing countries. Changes in those rates are apt to react on British domestic interest rates.

(7) Through competing with foreign sterling bonds in London. Having regard to the present extent of foreign investors' preference for dollar bonds, the differential in favour of dollar bonds is remarkably narrow. This is because of the local demand for sterling bonds by U.K. residents who are not permitted to acquire new dollar bonds except with the aid of investment dollars quoted at a high premium.

Domestic interest rates in European countries whose residents actually acquire European dollar bonds as investments, whether or not those bonds were issued in their countries, are affected in the following ways:

(1) Through competing with alternative domestic long-term investment facilities. While primarily it is the existing foreign dollar bonds already available in Europe

that are affected, if the amount of the new issues is large and the local bond market is relatively narrow, long-term interest rates in general might be affected.

(2) Through the effect on short-term interest rates of demand for credit facilities for a temporary financing of dollar bond issues.

(3) Through the effect of Euro-dollar or other Euro-currency rates of borrowing Euro-currency deposits for the temporary financing of Euro-bond issues, or their use for financing permanently investments in such bonds, or through replacement of Euro-dollar deposits by dollar bonds as investments by their owners.

(4) Through the effect on exchange rates. To the extent to which pressure is diverted from the dollar it is diverted to some other currency whose weakness is liable to lead to higher local interest rates if the monetary authorities concerned defend their exchange by means of higher interest rates or credit restrictions.

(5) Through repercussions of the effect on interest rates in the United States, in the issuing countries and in borrowing countries.

Finally, we must examine the effect on the domestic interest structure in the borrowing countries themselves. This effect tends to be more pronounced than those on domestic interest rates in the United States, in issuing countries or in investing countries, because the chances are that the amounts involved represent a larger percentage of the borrowing countries' total capital market resources. Their interest rates are influenced in the following ways:

(1) Through increasing the volume of capital and through competing with local lenders. In countries which are particularly short of capital the effect of borrowing abroad is apt to be particularly pronounced.

(2) Through enabling the monetary authorities to expand credit if the loan proceeds are acquired by the Central Bank, either direct from the borrower or through purchases in the foreign exchange market undertaken

to prevent the national currency from appreciating above its maximum support point or above any level at which the authorities want to hold it.

(3) Through the effect on domestic interest rates of an appreciation of the borrowing country's spot or forward exchange resulting from the sale of the proceeds and from the confidence inspired by an increase of the official reserve.

(4) Through the effect on Euro-dollar rates produced by a reduction of demand for Euro-dollar deposits.

(5) Through repercussions of the effect on interest rates in the United States, in issuing countries and in investing countries.

Possibly as and when the expansion in the turnover in the Euro-issues gathers momentum a stage may be reached at which it would become capable of affecting long-term interest rates to an extent comparable to the effect of Euro-dollar rates on short-term interest rates.

For several years, right until the series of crises triggered off by the devaluation of sterling in 1967, the Euro-bond market assisted the American authorities in their effort to keep down domestic interest rates. The reduction of foreign demand for American long-term capital kept down the extent to which the dollar had to be defended by means of high interest rates and credit restrictions. From 1968, however, in spite of the increase in American borrowing in the Euro-bond market, it ceased to be possible to avoid higher domestic interest rates in the United States.

CHAPTER TWELVE

Deutsche Mark Issues

WE saw in Chapter 4 that the Euro-bond market had originated essentially as a dollar bond market. There were, however, from an early stage, issues also in other denominations. But the Swiss franc, which has commanded high respect for an uninterrupted period of over three decades, has not played a prominent part in the Euro-issue market, owing to the Swiss Government's strong opposition to its use as an international currency. The French franc, which was very strong for several years in the 'sixties until the disturbances of 1968, was prevented from playing a prominent part by exchange control until its relaxation in 1967 and thereafter by fears of a restoration of exchange control – fears which came to materialise in 1968 – as well as by various handicaps to large-scale foreign issues.

As for sterling, it came to be disqualified from serving as the currency of Euro-bond issues – as distinct from bond issues by borrowers of the Sterling Area and of a few other countries admitted to the London capital market – owing to the frequently recurrent sterling crises. In a small number of instances Euro-bonds with a sterling D. mark option provision were issued. Even though investors subscribed to such issues almost entirely because of their implicit confidence in D. marks, many of them regarded the option to claim payment in sterling as an additional marginal attraction, partly for sentimental reasons for old times' sake and partly in the vague hope that some day sterling might yet regain its long-lost strength and prestige. There were also a number of composite unit of account loans, to be dealt with in Chapter 13.

Although U.S. dollars are still by far the most important currency in terms of which Euro-bonds are issued, the relative importance of D. mark issues increased considerably during the late 'sixties, especially in 1968–69. Out of a total of Euro-bond issues of $3,130 m. in 1968, $2,361 m. were issued in terms of dollars. But D. mark issues were next in importance. The equivalent of $662 m. was issued in terms of D. marks, compared with $148 m. in 1967 and $146 m. in 1966. This spectacular increase in 1968 was due in part to the remarkable improvement of the German balance of payments which induced the German Government to adopt measures to encourage the issue of foreign loans; in part to the heavy influx of foreign 'hot money', much of which was seeking employment in a lucrative form without getting out of D. marks; and in part to the growing willingness of German investors to acquire and hold foreign D. mark bonds.

There was much demand for D. mark bonds by non-residents in Germany for the purpose of speculating on a revaluation of the D. mark. But the temptation to engage in such speculation is apt to be overrated. Many speculators who expect a revaluation in the relatively near future are not unaware that it would be followed by wholesale profit-taking by those who, like themselves, had acquired foreign D. mark bonds solely for the purpose of trying to benefit by the revaluation. Such holders might easily lose on the fall of Euro-bond prices much of the profit they would make on the revaluation. Since they are prevented from holding German domestic D. mark securities by the 25 per cent tax on foreign holdings, they might prefer to hold their D. marks in a liquid form and employ them in the Euro-D. mark market.

An appreciable proportion of Euro-bonds issued in terms of D. marks is undoubtedly held by non-residents. Until recently they subscribed practically the whole of D. mark Euro-bond issues, and they are still actively encouraged to do so by the German Government through exempting foreign D. mark bonds from the 25 per cent withholding tax. But an increasing proportion of Euro-bond issues in terms of D. marks has been acquired by West German residents. Other German investors who do not expect a devaluation of the dollar or a revaluation of the D. mark, or who assume that a dollar devaluation would be part of an all-round devaluation or would be followed by an all-round devaluation of all currencies including the D. mark, acquire dollar Euro-bonds, partly for the sake of the interest differential which is about 1 per cent at the time of writing. The prospects of a further rise in Wall Street, through which German holders of convertible bonds would stand to benefit to an extent that would compensate them for a loss through a D. mark revaluation, provides additional attraction. But above all, the uncomfortable proximity of an increasingly aggressive Soviet Russia induces many West Germans to play for safety by holding dollar Euro-bonds of non-European countries, deposited in New York.

For the first time since 1914, Germany resumed in 1958 her rôle as a market for foreign issues. A D. mark issue of the Anglo-American Corporation was placed there. It was followed next year by a D. mark bond issue by the International Bank for Reconstruction and Development. But for several years in the 'sixties Germany remained a net importer of long-term capital in spite of her favourable balance of payments. This was because of the high long-term interest rates obtainable on German domestic bond issues in the domestic capital market. Their high yield attracted foreign investors, all the more so as there was no need for them to hedge against a devaluation risk. Foreign investors, in addition to benefiting by the high interest rates, had the choice between covering the forward exchange on their D. mark investments at a profit – forward D. marks have been at a premium for many years – or speculating on the possibility of a capital gain as a result of another revaluation of the D. mark following on its 5 per cent revaluation in 1961.

It was not until the German Government came to impose a 25 per cent withholding tax on interest and dividend payments to non-resident holders of German domestic securities that the paradoxical 'uphill' flow of capital from deficit countries to a surplus country became reversed. Even then the immediate effect of the new tax was an actual accentuation of the perverse trend. Heavy selling of German securities by foreign holders caused a fall in their prices and a rise in their yield. As a result it became worth while for German firms to borrow abroad through Luxembourg or other continental centres. So the measure which meant to discourage the unwanted influx of foreign capital actually encouraged it for some time.

Some former foreign holders of German securities reinvested in Euro-bonds the proceeds of their realised investments. Whether they preferred this to keeping the proceeds in D. mark in a liquid form depended largely on the reason why they had originally invested in D. marks. If it had been for the sake of benefiting by a revaluation it would not have suited their purpose to switch into dollar bonds, and it took years before an adequate selection of D. mark Euro-bond issued came to be available. But if the flight into D. marks was mainly fear of a devaluation of their own currencies, or some fiscal or political reason, the acquisition of dollar Euro-bonds might have appeared to them an acceptable solution. Many of them definitely preferred D. mark Euro-bonds, and it was their demand for such bonds which came to encourage the issue of Euro-bonds in that denomination. It provided an opportunity for German banks to participate increasingly in international syndicates engaged in the issue of Euro-bonds. Interest rates on those issues were not competitive, however, with the yields obtainable on German domestic bonds. Hence the initial reluctance of German investors to interest themselves in D. mark Euro-issues.

Owing to the spectacular expansion of the German economy, the German industrial demand for long-term capital was running high during the 'fifties and the 'sixties. In addition, the public authorities were also borrowers on a large scale. Last but by no means least, feverish building activity which continued long after the reconstruction of war damage was completed, gave rise to persistent demand for capital which was met mainly through the issue of long-term mortgage bonds. More will be said about the importance of that method of borrowing from the point of view of Germany's capacity to lend abroad.

After a temporary setback in the flow of D. mark Euro-bond

issues – as in the issue of Euro-bonds in general – during 1966, which continued in the case of D. mark issues in 1967 owing to deflationary measures in pursuit of the 'stop-go-stop' policy, their total showed a remarkable increase in 1968. This was largely due to the decline of domestic interest rates and the simultaneous increase of Euro-bond interest rates. The growing practice of issuing convertible bonds also attracted additional types of German investors as well as non-resident investors with funds in Germany. Even though the overwhelming majority of convertible bonds were dollar bonds, the possibility of capital gains induced many Germans to overcome their reluctance to invest abroad and in terms of a foreign currency.

One of the great advantages of the German capital market lies in its complete freedom from any restrictions on the export of capital. There are no restrictions, official or unofficial, on investment by German residents in Euro-bonds. Nor are there moral inhibitions of any kind. Quite on the contrary, the German authorities positively welcome private lending abroad, as it assists them in their task of dealing with the awkward problems created by Germany's *embarras de richesse*.

The spirit of economic liberalism which characterised Britain's attitude throughout the 19th century and right up to 1914, and also during part of the inter-war period, came to be inherited by the United States for some two decades between the end of the second World War and the adoption of the Interest Equalisation Tax. It now seems to have been inherited by West Germany. This is only natural. Economic liberalism – whether in the form of free trade in goods or free international movements of capital – is a luxury which only countries in a very strong position can afford. With her large export surpluses and increasing reserves, Germany is now in a position not to have to worry about any temporary over-lending, and she can play the part of an international financial market, not only by lending other nations' money but also by lending her own money – always provided that the German investing public will acquire increasingly and permanently the habit of sub-scribing and holding foreign securities.

The German banks have taken full advantage of the change in the situation brought about by the strength of the D. mark, the liberal policies of the German Government, the influx of foreign capital seeking reinvestment, and the growing willingness of the German investor to take an interest in Euro-bonds. Nowadays German banks participate in most international syndicates engaged in issuing Euro-bonds, and in 1968 the Deutsche Bank came to head the list of the banks which participated in the management of internationally syndicated Euro-bond issues. The German Government encourages their participation. The only restriction imposed on the placing of Euro-bond issues in Germany is that, if the bonds are in terms of D. marks the issuing syndicate has to be headed by a German bank. As the German banker Dr Wilfried Guth pointed out in a recent article in the *Zeitschrift für Langfristige Finanzierung*, the object of this condition is not to restrict capital movements but to retain control of the use of the D. mark as an international currency.

In a number of instances during 1968 D. mark Euro-bonds were issued in Germany exclusively by German banks or by banking groups consisting exclusively of German banks. They were able to do so partly because of the increase in their foreign deposits and partly because their German clients are now more willing to subscribe to such issues. By far the larger part of these issues, and also of D. mark issues with the participation of foreign banks, consisted of straight bonds for foreign Governments or international institutions. With the exception of 1966 when the issue of convertible bonds by the German subsidiary of Texas Oil in exchange for Deutsche Erdöl A.G. shares raised the total of D. mark Euro-bond issue to $237·7 m. the totals of convertible D. mark bond issues were in every year a bare fraction of those of straight bonds.

Borrowers in terms of D. marks included international institutions such as the Bank for Reconstruction and Development, the European Investment Bank, the European Coal and Steel Community and the Inter-American Development Bank. They included a number of foreign Governments such as those of the Scandinavian States, Austria, the Argentine, Venezuela, Japan, South Africa and Mexico, and even Commonwealth Governments, Australia and New Zealand. There were a number of municipal issues for Vienna, Copenhagen, Helsinki, Yokohama, Kobe, etc., and a number of loans for French, Italian and other Government-controlled institutions, or issues of unofficial corporations under the guarantees of their respective Governments. During 1968 a feature of Euro-issue activity was issues of D. mark bonds for French official institutions – an example followed in 1969 by the British Gas Council.

From the borrowers' point of view the issue of bonds in terms of D. marks entails a risk arising from the possibility of a revaluation of the D. mark as well as from the possibility of a devaluation of the borrower's own currency. But the interest differential is attractive, and if a second revaluation of the D. mark should not exceed 5 per cent, the saving of 1 per cent p.a. would more than cover a capital loss on the loan and the higher interest cost for 15 to 20 years in terms of the borrower's currency.

Apart altogether from the advantage of the lower interest rate, more borrowers are likely to be tempted to risk a revaluation loss mainly because of the easier availability of D. mark loans as and when German domestic investment demand for Euro-bonds in local currency will expand. It is not safe, however, to assume that the expanding trend of the German capital market for Euro-issues would necessarily continue uninterrupted. Although the revival of the long-lost German habit of investing abroad points in that direction, we must bear in mind the possibility of a reaction through defaults by debtors, or through a further increase of domestic requirement which enjoy a *de facto* priority over requirements of foreign borrowers, or even through changes in the official policy.

As German lending has been confined largely to acquiring bonds of borrowers of high standing, wholesale defaults are unlikely, except in case of wars or of major economic crises. On the other hand, an increase in domestic demand for capital which would drive up German long-term interest rates and would pre-empt German supplies of long-term capital is always a possibility, even though the German authorities are determined to prevent a runaway boom. They themselves are not likely to change their liberal attitude towards foreign borrowing, unless Germany should develop a substantial and persistent adverse balance of payments.

Even then the possibility of political reactions to a policy of discouraging American borrowing in Germany is liable to influence the Government's attitude to a considerable degree. Germany could not afford, from a politico-military point of view, to place the United States in a position in which she and her Allies are compelled for financial considerations to withdraw their forces stationed in Germany. Presumably it has been partly for this reason that Germany has abstained from following the French example by converting her dollars into gold. It has been partly for this reason that the German authorities have been trying their best to mitigate the adverse effects of the German export surplus and the influx of foreign funds.

The extent to which Germany will be able to absorb Eurobonds will depend largely on its domestic requirements of long-term capital. This again depends largely on the amounts absorbed by issues of mortgage bonds. The full importance of this factor is indicated by the fact that the total of all outstanding mortgage bonds in Germany amounted until recently to more than half of the total of all outstanding German securities. Should Germany continue to prosper – and there appears to be no reason to doubt that she will – her prosperity would continue to manifest itself in increasing building activity, absorbing increasing amounts of her long-term capital resources.

It may well be asked, is it absolutely necessary that this building activity should be financed in a way that is fated to keep down the amount available for investment abroad? This aspect of Germany's ability and willingness to re-lend abroad her large export surpluses has received remarkably little attention. Yet it is obvious that if Germany should continue to finance mortgages by means of long-term bond issues they

E

are bound to pre-empt her capital resources and prevent a really adequate expansion of her market for foreign loans. Under the British system mortgages are financed mainly out of resources provided by short-term deposits with building societies. This system has been found to be satisfactory, and there is no reason why Germany should not consider its adoption to an increasing degree, so as to make room for more foreign issues in her capital market. The German Government could and should encourage such a change. A high proportion of German *Hypothekenbanken* is controlled by various German State and Municipal authorities, and even privately-owned mortgage banks could be encouraged to adopt the method of short-term financing by the provision of Government guarantees. By such means many thousands of millions of D. marks could be made available year after year for lending abroad. The problems arising from Germany's persistently favourable balance of payments and her increasing gold and foreign exchange reserves could thus be solved.

If Germany continues to progress from strength to strength in the international monetary and financial sphere, the impact of her capital market on the trend of interest rates on Euro-bonds would increase in strength. A change in the German method of mortgage financing might result in a perceptible all-round decline in Euro-bond interest rates as a result of Germany's increased capacity to absorb such bonds. The effect of such a change on foreign exchanges would be even more significant, because it would neutralise the disturbing effect of the German export surpluses on the international movement of short-term funds and on speculative activity.

It is well to remember that the reason in the past why the strength of sterling did not produce any international disturbing effect similar to that produced by the present strength of the D. mark was Britain's ability and willingness to re-lend the surplus instead of accumulating it either in the form of an abnormally larger gold reserve or in the form of short-term claims on foreign countries.

In the absence of an adequate expansion of German long-term lending abroad the volume of Euro-D. mark deposits and their importance in the Euro-currency market would continue to increase. Although much of them would be absorbed by non-resident subscribers to D. mark Euro-bond issues, these loans would not mop up anything like the total of the influx of foreign funds encouraged by the perennial balance of payment surpluses. Indeed if continued inflation in the United States is combined with resistance to pressure in favour of a devaluation of the dollar, a stage might be reached when D. marks would become the most important Euro-currency instead of Euro-dollars, and the principal currency in terms of which Euro-bonds would be issued.

Meanwhile the expansion of the absorbing capacity of the German capital market for Euro-bond issues tends to support the dollar quite considerably, through the reversal of the rôles of Germany and the United States in respect of their borrower-lender relationship. On the other hand, increase in the proportion of subscriptions to Euro-bond issues in D. marks instead of dollars tends to reduce the demand for dollars by subscribers. To the extent to which the German capital market lends in D. marks to countries other than the United States, the increase of Euro-bond issues tends to be detrimental to the dollar.

CHAPTER THIRTEEN

Composite Unit of Account Loans

HITHERTO this book was primarily concerned with foreign lending in the form of bonds issued in Europe in demoninations of U.S. dollars and, to a less extent, in denominations of D. marks. An account of the system of Euro-issues would not be complete, however, without describing and examining the main alternative systems – the issue of loans in the form of multiple currency bonds, parallel issues and, above all, composite unit of account bonds. The latter in particular deserves much attention, partly because it is actually in operation to a noteworthy extent, and partly because it is an imaginative experiment with interesting possibilities.

The idea of some form of international money has long tempted imaginative economists and has given rise to various schemes for the creation of currencies circulating in many countries, or at any rate universally accepted in international payments. The international unit of account with which we are concerned in this chapter has no such ambitious scope. The bankers who have created it and any who are applying it in practice do not mean it to become a currency in which foreign trade would ever be actually transacted as distinct from using the device for loans financing trade, domestic or foreign. Even less do the authors of the device envisage it as the world currency of the future.

Nevertheless, in one respect the authors of the scheme have succeeded where more ambitious monetary reformers have failed so far – their device is actually in use. Most other suggestions, with the notable exception of Special Drawing Rights, may never be put in practice. Success or failure of the experiment with composite units of account is, however, liable to improve the chances of bolder experiments in the direction of international currency.

Ever since 1957 Continental banks have been experimenting with loan contracts containing some form of 'multiple currency clause' under which holders have the option of claiming payment of interest and repayment of principal in any one of several currencies, on the basis of a fixed exchange rate between them – usually their gold or dollar parities that is in force at the time of the issue. For instance, in 1957 a Belgian oil company issued in Canada, Switzerland, Belgium, Germany and Holland a 20-year loan of $25 million containing a clause providing for payment in guilders, D. marks, Swiss francs or Belgian francs at a fixed exchange rate at the bondholders' option. This transaction was followed by a number of others based on the same principle. But the formula was not looked upon as satisfactory by many borrowers. Those in a position to refuse to sign on the dotted line declined it because it would mean that, should any one of the currencies of the contract be revalued, all bondholders would claim payment in that currency. The debtor would suffer a loss, without a corresponding chance to gain by devaluation unless all the currencies of the contract were devalued. A devaluation of the debtors' own currency would mean a corresponding increase in the burden of his debt.

A mitigated form of currency option enables investors to choose between several currencies at the time when the loan is issued. Once he has made his choice, however, he is not in a position to alter it. This formula does not entail anything like the same risk for the borrower as the multiple currency clause. Nor does it provide anything like the same safeguard for the lender.

Dr Hermann Abs, head of the Deutsche Bank, advocated the issue of 'parallel' loans in several national tranches each of which would be in the currency of the market in which it is issued. The interest rate on all tranches would be uniform, but the issue prices would vary according to the conditions prevailing in the various markets. Although the plan has its good points it does not seem to have been received favourably. It would not solve the problem of integrating the European capital markets, because bonds issued in terms of various European currencies would be judged by investors according to the view they take of the currencies in which they are issued, and price differentials would tend to remain.

One of the difficulties of parallel issues would be the difficulty of synchronising their issue. Owing to the discrepancies between regulations in various countries relating to new issues of foreign bonds, and also between the actual application of those regulations in practice, there may have to be time lags of a month or more between the various issues, and meanwhile interest rates are liable to change.

Having regard to the disadvantages of the various alternative schemes, it is not surprising that the formula of issuing bonds in terms of composite units of account should meet with favourable response. It was first put forward by a Belgian banker, M. F. Collin, and was first applied in actual practice in 1961. It seeks to reconcile the conflicting interests of borrowers and lenders. Loans issued in terms of composite units of account differ from multiple currency loans in that the creditor has no option to choose among the 'reference currencies' but has to be content with receiving payment in that of these currencies which has not appreciated or depreciated, or which has depreciated or appreciated to the least extent. This formula reduces to a minimum losses debtors are liable to suffer through revaluations, because the list of reference currencies contains some which are most unlikely to be revalued. It also reduces to a minimum losses lenders are liable to suffer through devaluations, because some of the reference currencies are unlikely to be devalued. It seeks to ensure that payment of interest and repayment of capital is made in a monetary unit whose gold value corresponds as nearly as possible to that of the one in which the loan was made.

The composite unit of account is based on the system elaborated under the European Payments Union Scheme in 1950 for the purpose of clearing debit and credit items between members of the Union through the Bank for International

Settlements. Details of the EPU system are highly involved and need not concern us here, especially as its use was discontinued with the termination of the EPU. M. Collin's formula took over from the EPU system the list of reference currencies which formed the basis of loan contracts. Details of the actual application of this formula vary from issue to issue, but the fundamental rule that, while the currency in which the debtor has to discharge payments is left to the choice of the creditor, the exchange rate on the basis of which payment is made in the currency chosen must be the one which is the nearest to the original exchange parities as defined in the contract, is embodied in all contracts. Under that formula creditors would not benefit by revaluations unless and until all seventeen currencies have been revalued and even them payment would be made on the basis of the currency which was revalued to the smallest extent. In the absence of changes in the legal parities, or if floating exchange rates are adopted, payment would be based on the basis of the currency which appreciated to the smallest extent.

In their turn, debtors could only benefit by devaluation if all seventeen currencies were devalued or depreciated, and even then this benefit would be based on the devaluation or depreciation of the currency which was devalued or which depreciated to the smallest extent.

If only some of the reference currencies are revalued or devalued, the payment in the currency chosen by the bondholders has to be reckoned on the basis of the exchange rate of one of the currencies which are not revalued or devalued. So long as there remains one single reference currency out of the seventeen which is not revalued or devalued, or which, in the absence of legal changes in its parity, has not depreciated or appreciated, debtors are safeguarded against abnormal exchange loss and are deprived of exchange profit. This formula does not provide an absolutely watertight safeguard for investors against a devaluation of the currency of the investment, but devaluation risk is greatly reduced. Indeed it could not be reduced even more without the application of some provision which would amount to a gold clause pure and simple. On the other hand, prospects of a revaluation profit are also reduced to a minimum. Non-speculative investors gladly pay that price for the safeguard against devaluation.

The formula does not of course safeguard debtors against the risk of a loss through a devaluation of their own currency, nor does it deprive debtors of profit through a revaluation of their own currency. If the debtors' own currency is one of the seventeen reference currencies the only situation in which, in case of a devaluation or revaluation of all currencies, it becomes the currency of the payments under the loan contract is if the extent of its change is smaller than that of all other reference currencies. Otherwise payments have to be made in another currency, in which case the debtor benefits by an appreciation of his currency in terms of that currency and suffers a loss through a depreciation of his own currency in terms of that currency. The rule applies in reverse to creditors and their currencies. The formula does not safeguard them from loss through a revaluation of their own currency, nor does it deprive them of profits from a devaluation of their own currency, unless their currency becomes the currency of the payments under the loan contract.

Complications arise if some of the seventeen currencies are devalued while others are revalued. Under the original formula some anomalous situations were liable to arise. If, for instance, sixteen reference currencies were devalued substantially while one was revalued slightly, payment would be made on the basis on the one revalued currency, in conformity with the provision that the payment has to be based on the value of the reference currency whose departure from the basic parities is the smallest. Conversely, if sixteen currencies were drastically revalued while the seventeenth moderately devalued, creditors would suffer a disadvantage, because payment would be made on the basis of the lower value of the one devalued currency, even if that currency were the least important among the reference currencies.

A more equitable formula has therefore been adopted, according to which the unit of account has to be changed only if all seventeen reference currencies have been either devalued or revalued, and it has to be changed in the same direction in which two-thirds of the currencies have changed, but only to the extent of the change in the currency that has changed to the least extent in that direction. This means that if at least twelve out of the seventeen currencies have been changed in the same direction while five or fewer currencies have been changed in the opposite direction, the currency whose new value must form the basis of payments is the one of the majority which has changed to the smallest extent.

This solution is far from being ideal. For one thing, it is not applied if eleven or less currencies are changed in the same direction, even though such a situation would result in the application of the self-same absurd anomalous solution that has been criticised above. The formula is also criticised for being complicated and unintelligible far beyond the understanding of the ordinary investor who has to make up his mind on its merits and demerits in order to decide whether to acquire and hold bonds based on it. Finally, it has also been criticised on the ground that some of the seventeen reference currencies are quite unimportant. Their inclusion is said to be at best irrelevant and at worst detrimental to the interests of creditors or debtors. The validity of this latter criticism may best be judged by glancing at the following list of the reference currencies that gives their parities or 'basic values':

One unit of account was equal, at the beginning of 1969, to one U.S. dollar and to:

> 26.000 Austrian schillings
> 50.000 Belgian francs
> 7.500 Danish kroner
> 4.93706 French francs
> 4.000 German D. marks
> 0.416667 pounds sterling
> 30.000 Greek drachmae
> 88.100 Icelandic kroner
> 0.416667 Irish pounds
> 625.000 Italian lire

50.000 Luxembourg francs
3.620 Netherlands guilders
7.14286 Norwegian kroner
28.750 Portuguese escudos
5.17321 Swedish kronor
4.37282 Swiss francs
9.000 Turkish pounds

All these parities are identical with those of the U.S. dollar in relation to the seventeen currencies at the beginning of 1969, so that the composite unit of account is equal to one gold dollar at its weight and fineness as fixed in 1934. But a change in the gold content of the dollar would not affect the above list of parities, for, in the absence of provisions to the contrary, the unit of account would continue to be based on the quantity of gold represented by the dollar since its devaluation in 1934 – 0.88867088 grammes of fine gold. But if, as seems probable, a dollar devaluation should be followed by simultaneous or successive devaluations of all reference currencies it would affect the gold value of the currency in which payment must be made, as it would become adjusted to the value of the reference currency the devaluation of which would be of the smallest extent. For this reason, the multiple currency clause is not a gold clause, which is as well, for gold clauses are invalid and even prohibited in some countries.

The prices of unit account bonds would be affected by trends of exchange rates if there appeared to be a possibility of changes in all parities. For instance, if a devaluation of all reference currencies were expected, the market would discount a deprecia- of the unit of account corresponding to the anticipated extent of the devaluation of the currency which would be devalued to the smallest degree. The prices of unit of account bonds would be similarly affected by an anticipation of a possible devalua- tion or revaluation of at least 12 out of the 17 reference currencies, and a possible change in the opposite sense of the remaining reference currencies. So long as one of the 17 currencies retains its old parities, payments would be based on the parity of that currency.

Obviously, the inclusion of currencies such as the Greek drachma or the Turkish pound reduces to vanishing point the chances of an all-round revaluation, so that to that extent at any rate the formula safeguards the interests of debtors. On the other hand, the inclusion of all Western European hard currencies reduces but certainly does not eliminate the likelihood of a devaluation of all reference currencies. An all-round devaluation of currencies under the auspices of the International Monetary Fund, either to a uniform degree as proposed by M. Rueff, or to a varying degree allowing for the extent of the respective overvaluations or undervaluations of the currencies, is in the long run rather more than a mere possibility. To the extent to which it is liable to occur, the safeguard of the interests of creditors is not watertight. Both creditors and debtors are liable to be affected by the provision under which a change in the currency of payment does not presuppose changes in all parities in the same direction. If, for instance, 12 softer currencies are devalued while the remaining 5 harder currencies are revalued, the value of the unit would be lowered to the extent of the reduction of the gold parity of the currency which departed to the smallest extent from the parities fixed in the contract.

The explanation of the inclusion of soft or unimportant currencies in the formula is that they had been included in the European Payments Union formula which had been endorsed by all participating countries. The maintenance of that formula in its original form – subject only to adjustments of parities as a result of devaluations and revaluations – gives therefore the unit of account based on it additional prestige and historical justification. As M. Collin pointed out, it greatly reduces the likelihood of legislation against its application in loan contracts in any of the seventeen countries concerned.

The objection of the Swiss authorities to the inclusion of the Swiss franc among the reference currencies was overcome as a result of an agreed compromise under which bondholders shall be entitled to be paid on the basis of the current exchange rate of the Swiss franc, but no actual payment must be made in that

currency. Bondholders have to indicate their second choice of
the reference currency in which the actual payment, reckoned
on the basis of the current exchange rate of the Swiss franc, is
to be made to them.

The attitude of the Swiss authorities is inspired by their
determination to resist an extension of the use of the Swiss franc
as an international currency. This attitude has obvious practical justification in so far as it aims at preventing the issue of
loans abroad in terms of Swiss francs, for interest rates on such
bonds necessarily compete with interest rates on similar issues
in the Swiss market. As we remarked before, any conceivable
total of dollar bonds issued abroad could never be more than a
small fraction of the total dollar bonds issues in the United
States. But in the case of Switzerland the relative proportion of
Swiss franc loans issued abroad to those issued in the domestic
market might well become uncomfortably high. Extensive use
of the Swiss franc, even if it be through its inclusion in multiple
currency clauses, or among reference currencies of unit of
account issues, might conceivably influence long-term interest
rates in Switzerland in a sense conflicting to official policy.
Many investors might well prefer such bonds to Swiss franc
bonds issued in the domestic market at lower interest rates.

Viewed from this angle, however, it seems that the Swiss
authorities, in agreeing to the compromise outlined above,
mistook the shadow for the substance. Investors who trust the
Swiss franc implicitly might be attracted by unit of account
bonds because under the new formula they are safeguarded
against devaluation at least to the same extent as if they
acquired Swiss franc bonds issued in Switzerland. It is true,
under the terms of the compromise Swiss francs cannot be used
in actual payment to bondholders. But there is nothing to
prevent those receiving payments in some other currency from
converting the amount received immediately into Swiss francs.
They would receive the same amount of Swiss francs (less a
small turn on the foreign exchange transaction) as if they had
been permitted to receive actual payment in Swiss francs direct
from the paying agents. In practice the paying agents may

themselves carry out the conversion, in which case the actual payment would be made in Swiss francs even if no paying agents can be appointed in Switzerland.

This compromise further complicated a formula which was criticised for being over-involved even before this additional complication. Should other countries follow the Swiss example the adoption of further compromises on different terms might well reduce the system to absurdity by making it entirely unintelligible to the average investors, or even to institutional investors who are usually the principal subscribers to unit of account issues.

In any case the system has yet to face its ultimate test consisting of its interpretation by law courts. Owing to its novelty and its complicated nature, it is believed in many quarters that it is almost certain to give rise to legal actions sooner or later. In case of unforseen contingencies legal battles would have to be fought out before Law Courts in a number of countries and new chapters would have to be added to textbooks on international law in respect of money and banking. The result of such legal battles, or the operation of the system over a prolonged period without giving rise to such lawsuits, will determine the definitive interpretation of the formula.

Subscribers to unit of account issues usually have the choice between paying in one of several currencies. This option does not extend over the full range of the seventeen reference currencies but is confined to the leading currencies.

Let us now examine the broader economic aspects of unit of account loans. In so far as they appeal to a class of borrowers, finance houses and investors who for some reason fight shy of internationl loans in terms of any existing currency, or in terms of any of the alternative formulas, the adoption of the new device is to be welcomed as an additional means for furthering the international redistribution of capital. So long as there are revaluation risks and devaluation risks any formula that reduces them is a welcome contribution to the solution of the problem. Time alone will show whether the contribution made by the composite unit of account formula will be able to assist to any considerable extent in the elimination of currency uncertainty as one of the main obstacles to international portfolio investment.

To the extent to which unit of account loans take the place of dollar loans the device tends to reduce the international use of the dollar. Until comparatively recently this might have influenced American opinion against such loans. As a result of experience during the late 'fifties and early 'sixties, it has come to be realised that the use of any one currency as an international currency has its disadvantages as well as its advantages and it would be a mistake to overrate the latter and ignore the former for misplaced considerations of prestige.

Our next task is to examine how unit of account loans affect the dollar and the other exchanges concerned. The view is widely held even in banking circles that loans issued in terms of units of account, or indeed in terms of any currency other than the dollar outside the United States, does not affect the dollar. After all, the loans are issued in the foreign market, they are not in U.S. dollar denominations, and they are lent by non-residents in the United States to non-residents in the United States. On the face of it the dollar does not come into it at all, unless American refugee funds are used by subscribers to unit of account loans and are exported for the purpose of acquiring unit of account loans. To some extent this might occur, since the unit of account formula provides a new kind of security which might possibly appeal to some American investors.

Appearances are often deceptive, however. As we pointed out already in Chapter 10, unit of account loans, as indeed loans issued in any currency other than the dollar, are liable to affect the dollar exchange. They can do so in the following ways:

(1) Holders of dollars (resident or non-resident) may sell dollars to buy the currency in which payment for the bonds have to be made.

(2) The issue or the acquisition of the bonds by investors may be financed with the aid of dollars borrowed in the United States.

(3) It may be financed with Euro-dollars. This tends to cause an increase in Euro-dollar rates.

(4) The proceeds may be spent on repaying debts owed in the United States.

(5) The proceeds may be spent on imports from the United States.

(6) The proceeds may be spent on non-American goods instead of importing American goods.

(7) The transaction may obviate the necessity to borrow in the United States.

From the above list it appears that the dollar is far from being immune from the effects of any fluctuations in the volume of unit of account issues, once such issues should reach a high proportion of the total. Indeed, in so far as they substitute buying of other currencies for buying of dollars by subscribers or by banks financing the issues, the effect of an expansion in the volume of such issues tends to be unfavourable to the dollar.

The transaction is liable to affect the exchanges of currencies of countries in which unit of account loans are issued or placed in the same way as they are affected by the issue of dollar loans. Likewise, in countries with exchange restrictions in which there is a special market for currencies that can be used by residents for subscribing or buying such bonds – such as the British market in investment currencies – they tend to affect the rate for such currencies in the same way as they are affected by the issue of dollar loans, about which more will be said in the next chapter.

If a sufficient number of unit of account loans is issued it will create a set of international interest rates which, in theory, is even more international than the yield on Euro-bond issues in dollars, because the latter is influenced, to some extent at any rate, by interest rates prevailing in the American bond market in general, and the American market for foreign bonds in particular. In practice, however, even the rates on unit of account issues will not be completely independent. For there is, at any given moment, a differential between Euro-bonds issued in terms of units of account and those issued in terms of dollars.

Since the latter are influenced in some measure by American domestic interests rates, the former are also liable to be affected by them indirectly.

For instance, if short-term interest rates in New York fall it becomes more advantageous for many foreign borrowers to secure credits in New York instead of issuing dollar bonds – assuming of course that there is no exchange control that deprives them of the choice. The resulting decline of borrowing in the form of dollar-bond issues will tend to lower their interest rates and this again will tend to lower interest rates on unit of account bonds. Lower short-term interest rates in New York might divert into that market some borrowers who would otherwise have borrowed by means of issuing unit of account bonds.

One of the economic advantages of the market in dollar Euro-bonds is that, in conjunction with the Euro-dollar market they have established a very useful communicating channel between long-term and short-term loans. Long Euro-dollar deposits and short Euro-bond issues between them have created much-needed medium-term facilities. It is conceivable that such a market will develop in unit of account loans. There are actual instances of Euro-currency deposits in terms of composite units of account. This system is still in its infancy at the time of writing, but it has distinct possibilities. If and when it comes to be applied systematically it would encourage the further development of the market in unit of account bonds.

It appears that, as far as the effect of unit of account loans on exchanges and interest rates are concerned, we are if anything even more in the realm of conjecture than in respect of the effects of dollar Euro-bond issues. Should a really active market develop in unit of account loans, their interest rates might well become an important factor affecting not only other international interest rates but even domestic interest rates. This may become particularly the case concerning interest rates in smaller countries. Hence the determination of the Swiss authorities not to allow the Swiss franc to become the dominant reference currency in unit of account loans.

Recent contracts of unit of account loans provide for the hypothetical situation that might arise if gold were to be demonetised in all seventeen countries whose currencies are used as reference currencies – that is, if all 17 currencies should cease to have an official gold parity. Such a situation might conceivably arise if all the countries concerned should decide to adopt the system of floating exchanges. Under provisions embodied in some loan contracts in such a situation the value of the unit of account would be related to 'the most stable currency', i.e., the currency the exchange rate of which, in relation to the 16 other reference currencies as quoted on the last day before the last of the 17 currencies ceased to have a gold parity, varied to the least extent from its gold parity that was in force on the last day on which it still had a gold parity. The value of the unit of account, on the basis of which debtors are bound to pay interest and principal, would then be based on the gold parity of the last currency still on a gold basis, as it was on the last day prior to its suspension.

This formula is rather involved. In substance it means that if all reference currencies ceased to have gold parities the value of the unit of account would be determined by the gold parity of the currency which was the last to abandon its gold parity. This means that even in the event of a return to currency chaos similar to the one experienced during the 'thirties, holders of unit of account bonds are safeguarded in theory against the resulting wild fluctuations, as their payments would be reckoned on the basis of the gold parity of one of the reference currencies. Whether in practice the rule would be upheld or abolished, as the gold clause was abolished after the United States suspended the gold standard in 1933, is of course anybody's guess. It will probably depend on the number and relative importance of Euro-bonds with unit of accounts clauses on the lines indicated above. If such issues remained exceptional it might not be deemed worth while to legislate about them, as Britain did not deem it worth while to legislate about gold clauses in the 'thirties, owing to the small number of contracts with such a clause.

CHAPTER FOURTEEN

American Borrowing

HAVING played the part of the principal provider of long-term loans to Europe for half a century from 1914, in war and in peace, the United States curtailed that role in 1964 and reversed it in 1968 when she became a borrower in Europe on a large scale. Out of total Euro-bonds of over $3,000 million issued during that year, more than $1,800 million was on behalf of American borrowers. All of it was on account of corporations and most of it assumed the form of convertible bonds.

The increase of American borrowing in Europe gave rise to much criticism on the ground that, in addition to discontinuing its activity of lending to Europe, the United States is now engaged in pre-empting European capital resources badly needed in Europe itself and on other continents. Such criticism overlooks the fact that the bulk of the American loans issued in Europe is for the purpose of financing American subsidiaries in Europe or elsewhere outside the United States. The reason why there was a sharp increase in Euro-bond issues during 1968 was that, as from the beginning of that year, it became compulsory for American firms to borrow abroad the capital required for their expansion abroad.

In any case, the United States has rendered Western Europe an immense service by compelling it to cease to depend forever on New York for its capital requirements. When in 1947 Mr Snyder, Secretary of the United States Treasury in the Truman Administration, paid a visit to London, I suggested to him that the best way in which his country could help my country would be by amending the American Constitution to prohibit any further financial assistance to Britain in time of peace. For it is reasonable to assume that, once the British people were made to realise that they could no longer depend on American support, they would put their backs into a supreme effort to work out their own salvation unaided. The same is presumably true to a varying degree of other Western European nations. So long as the United States continued to supply Europe with long-term capital no European capital market could develop.

Experience has strikingly confirmed the above assumption. The remarkable success of the efforts made by the Western European countries since 1964 to develop a capital market of their own showed that, once they came to realise that they could no longer depend on the New York market, they easily solved their problem. Nothing could illustrate better the success of their effort to that end than the fact that the newly-reconstructed European capital market is now in a position to lend on a large scale even to the United States.

The post-war physical and economic reconstruction of Western Europe was more or less completed by the late 'fifties and there was no longer any valid reason why it should not revive its capital-issuing activities. After all, European bankers are no less intelligent or enterprising in the sphere of international finance than American bankers, and there are many of them with first-hand pre-war experience in the handling of foreign loans. To a limited extent the Western European centres actually resumed the issue of such loans for the benefit of certain borrowers. Capital resources available for long-term lending were accumulating in spite of the creeping inflation that tended to discourage personal savings. It is true, in most European countries exchange control prevented long-term lending of local capital abroad. But several European countries attracted large amounts of foreign funds that became available for that purpose.

In spite of this, until 1964 many European borrowers of long-term capital satisfied most of their capital requirements in the New York market. The law of inertia, and possibly inferiority-complex due to the early post-war weakness of European currencies, prevented European banking centres from trying to develop similar markets even on a smaller scale.

In any case none of them was strong enough in isolation, and there was no attempt to combine their strength. So Western European countries continued not only to abstain from lending to other countries on any substantial scale but even to borrow from the United States. It was not until they found themselves forced by the new American policy to try to make Europe self-supporting in respect of its requirements of long-term capital that they made a long-overdue effort to achieve that end. Western Europe became independent of American long-term lending, not through a ban on financial assistance on the lines I had suggested to Mr Snyder in 1947, but through the adoption of the Interest Equalisation Tax which made it unprofitable for American investors to acquire European securities.

The United States initiated in the middle 'sixties a chain of developments that has led to the emergence of remarkably efficient capital markets in a number of European financial centres and the combination of their resources through close co-operation in the issue and subsequent marketing of foreign loans. She went a step further in the late 'sixties by actually becoming a borrower in the European market on an impressive scale. On the face of it, once more, as before 1914, Europe seems to be providing the United States with long-term capital.

In reality there has been no basic reversal of the Eastward trend of international capital movements across the Atlantic. For while the United States has become the largest borrower in Europe – not only through issues of convertible Euro-bonds but also through borrowing Euro-dollars in London and elsewhere – she has continued to supply Europe with long-term capital in the form of direct investment by establishing branch factories or acquiring controlling interest in European industrial concerns. What is happening is that the export of American capital for direct investment is financed, directly or indirectly, through American long-term and short-term borrowing abroad.

New York did not suspend its foreign lending activities altogether. As we saw earlier, bonds of a number of non-European countries are exempted from the Interest Equalisation Tax and are in a position to issue bonds in New York instead of, or in addition to, borrowing in Europe. Most Euro-bonds issued in terms of dollars are listed in Wall Street even though in present circumstances there are no dealings in them. Their listing has the advantage of giving investors the guarantee that the detailed information required under the extremely stringent American regulations would be forthcoming. There is also a possibility of a removal of the Interest Equalisation Tax, so that dealing in Wall Street for U.S. residents would become possible. Moreover, American banks came to take an increasingly active interest in Euro-bond issues even though no part of them can be placed in the United States in present conditions, partly because they can place the bonds with their non-resident clients – including American affiliates abroad – and partly because the American borrowers are their clients. As for future prospects, the rise in American interest rates in the late 'sixties makes it appear possible, however, that even a removal of the Interest Equalisation Tax would not necessarily attract a flood of foreign bond issues to New York.

United States corporations have become very large borrowers of capital in Europe. This is due to some extent to the rise in interest rates in the United States, but even more to the tighter money conditions resulting from the measures adopted by the Washington Administration in defence of the dollar. But the most important influence was provided by the succession of 'guidelines' issued by the Johnson Administration, asking American corporations to meet their overseas capital require-ments by borrowing abroad. As we already pointed out, as from 1968 this has become compulsory.

There can be no doubt that, had it not been for the large number of American issues of convertible Euro-bonds during 1968, the balance of payments of the United States, instead of showing a nominal surplus, would have closed with a substantial deficit. As it is, it is open to argument whether the balancing, by means of Euro-bond issues, of a deficit on current trans-actions plus the export of capital for direct investment, can really be considered adequate, except from the point of view of balance of payments accountancy. But then, from that technical point of view all balances of payments must always balance by definition. Without borrowing in the Euro-bond market, the American deficit on current account and on long-term capital account would have been balanced as a result of an increase in American short-term indebtedness abroad, whether in the form of a further increase of foreign dollar holdings or in the form of additional Euro-dollar borrowing. Alternatively there would have been a further decline of the gold reserve. But there can be no doubt that the balancing of the deficit by medium- and long-term loans in Europe is a sounder method – or, to be more precise, a less unsound method – of balancing than the increase of external short-term liabilities or a further reduction of the gold reserve.

The 64-million dollar question is whether, from the point of view of the United States, it is likely to prove to be profitable to finance the acquisition of equity capital in Europe and else-where by means of issuing abroad bonds convertible into American equities. No such question would arise if direct investment abroad were financed by borrowing abroad in the form of straight bond issues. The decline of the burden of such foreign loans in real terms would almost certainly secure for the United States a substantial net gain through the apprecia-tion of the real assets abroad acquired with the aid of resources raised through issuing Euro-bonds abroad. But since the acquisition of direct investment has been financed very largely through the issue of convertible bonds giving foreign residents the option of acquiring American equities – albeit at prices well above the present quotations – the answer is more complicated. It depends largely on the view one takes, on the one hand, about the probable extent of capital gains on American shares to be obtained by holders of convertible bonds in spite of the investment premium and, on the other hand, on that of American gains on direct investment abroad.

For the time being American affiliates abroad and share-holdings in foreign firms probably give American holders a yield that bears comparison with the interest paid on American

Euro-bond issues prior to their conversion. Should industrial expansion abroad lag behind industrial expansion in the United States, the net capital gains made by European investors through converting their bonds into American shares might exceed the American capital gains on their foreign direct investments. In that case in spite of the 'safety-margin' for the benefit of the United States, represented by the conversion premium, the United States would suffer net capital loss. On the other hand, since industries as a whole outside the United States are less highly developed than those within the United States, there seems to be wider scope for their further development with the aid of American knowhow, so that the United States as a whole might earn more substantial capital gains on her non-American direct investment than would non-Americans on their American equity investments. This would justify from an American financial point of view the present policy of financing direct investments abroad by means of issuing convertible Euto-bonds.

But from a broad economic point of view as well as from a political point of view the expansion of American direct investment abroad, financed directly or indirectly by Euro-bond issues, is liable to entail grave disadvantages for the United States. By passing on American know-how to European and other industrial rival countries – American methods, once exported, are not likely to remain the monopoly of American affiliates abroad – the United States is assisting foreign competition. Even the affiliates that are under American control, if they want to work profitably, may have to acquire some of the actual or potential markets of their parent firms or of other industrial firms in the United States. Out of the proceeds of their sales only a small percentage will represent net profits which can be repatriated. This means that, even though at the time of writing the American balance of payments is effectively helped by borrowing abroad, in the long run it stands to lose on current account much of what it now gains on capital account. Whether or not such losses are liable to be offset, and considerably more than offset, by capital gains through an appreciation of the direct investments abroad is of course anybody's guess.

It is doubtful if many Americans realise that from a political point of view American industrial expansion abroad entails grave disadvantages and dangers to the United States. It explains, for instance, to a large degree President de Gaulle's anti-American attitude. In most countries the increase of American control over local industries is liable to generate a growing anti-American feeling. Symptoms of that feeling occurred even in Britain during 1967 and 1968 on occasions of strikes in American-controlled industrial concerns. To the ill-feeling caused by conflicts between employers and employees a great deal of ill-feeling due to the non-British nationality of the employers, and their unfamiliarity with British labour relations, came to be super-imposed. Yet Britain is undoubtedly the most pro-American country in Europe. In countries with a high proportion of Communist population, such as France and Italy, the temptation to nationalise American firms on more or less confiscatory terms might reinforce the political hostility of such populations towards the United States, and the immediate advantages that could be gained by such nationalisations might swell the ranks of the Communist parties. Even non-Communist public opinion resents the rapid growth of American control over local industries and regards it as a form of 'dollar imperialism' which is objected to all the more for being financed largely with European capital.

It is true, in Britain American-owned firms were exempted from steel nationalisation. Increased American participation in the British motor industry and in other key industries is causing resentment, however, and might strengthen opposition to continuing to exclude American firms from nationalisation.

By investing heavily in industries abroad, the United States is giving hostages to fortune. Owing to the decline of the American gold reserve and the increase of American short-term and long-term indebtedness abroad, it may no longer always be possible for the United States to rely on favourable treatment of American industrial interest in foreign countries in the expectation of future American financial assistance. Quite on the contrary, Governments of countries in which there is heavy American investment are in a position to bring pressure to bear on the United States by the threat of measures that would injure American subsidiaries. The more heavily the United States is committed in industrial investments in a foreign country the more heavily the dice are loaded against her.

On the other hand, in countries such as Britain and Germany an increase of American investment should be welcomed by non-Communist opinion for political reasons. It reinforces the necessity for the United States to give these countries her support in case of Soviet aggression. Although the same argument applies also in France and Italy, a large section of public opinion there does not want American protection against Soviet threats.

But, to return to our main subject after the above digression, it would be a mistake to believe that American borrowing in the Euro-bond market serves exclusively the purpose of financing American direct investment abroad. To a very large extent the proceeds of the loans are employed directly or indirectly by the parent firms themselves. In many instances the proceeds of the issues exceed the immediate requirements of the subsidiaries and the surplus is employed in the United States until the capital is needed abroad. Technical difficulties due to American legislation are overcome by borrowing through the intermediary of a subsidiary registered in the State of Delaware where special legislation is in force. The loans enable the subsidiaries to repatriate a higher proportion of their undistributed profits. In some instances the financing with the aid of foreign loans is retrospective – the parent firm recovers part of its own capital originally invested in the affiliate. Under various formulas, the parent firms borrow abroad for their own requirements as well as for those of the affiliates, largely owing to the credit squeeze in the United States.

Turning to the broader aspects of the use of the Euro-bond market by American borrowers, there is a great deal to be said for the new system under which international capital movements are no longer a one-way traffic. No country, not even one with the resources of the United States, should ever play the part of a modern Atlas carrying on its shoulders the financial burden of the entire Universe. It is to the advantage of the United States as well as of the rest of the world that there should be more than one capital market in which it is possible to borrow on a large scale.

The other side of the picture is that the facilities of the Euro-bond market can be misused. American corporations have been borrowing largely in order to comply with official policies enabling the United States Government to continue to abstain from applying the corrective measures that would have had to be taken in the absence of the capital resources borrowed abroad. Although this has brought temporary respite, in the long run the United States is liable to pay a heavy price for it.

From the point of view of American exports American borrowing cuts both ways. If it leads to direct investment abroad involving the export of capital goods from the United States, American export trade benefits by it. But if it mops up foreign-owned dollars which would have been spend otherwise on imports from the United States American exports are affected unfavourably.

From the point of view of the world economy, to the extent to which American borrowing obviates the need for even higher interest rates and credit squeeze in the United States, it relieves other countries from the necessity of adopting similar measures. Whether or not it would be to the advantage of the American economy to restore equilibrium by such measures in preference to devaluing the dollar, it is certainly to the advantage of Europe and of the rest of the world if the United States is not forced to adopt measures which are liable to react unfavourably on international financial markets and on world trade. Possibly in the absence of Euro-bond issues Americans would have borrowed even more Euro-dollars, forcing up interest rates to breaking point.

CHAPTER FIFTEEN

Convertible Bonds

ORIGINALLY the Euro-bond market confined itself to the issue of straight bonds of the conventional type, the borrowers being mostly Governments, Government-guaranteed institutions, municipalities, international institutions, and a limited number of business concerns of high standing. It simply assumed the rôle relinquished by the New York market when imposing Interest Equalisation Tax on the bond issues of a large number of countries. The late 'sixties witnessed, however, an innovation of outstanding importance. Euro-bond issues came to assume increasingly the form of convertible debentures.

In addition to being paid a fixed interest, holders of such convertible bonds are given an option to exchange their bonds for ordinary shares of the parent company of the borrowing firm which is usually a subsidiary company. That option can be exercised between two dates fixed in the loan contract, at a fixed price. The difference between the price of ordinary shares at the time of the issue of the bonds and the rate at which they can be converted is called the 'convertibility premium'.

The increasing popularity of convertible bonds may be judged by the fact that in 1964 only $72.5 million out of a total of Euro-bond issues of $857.3 million consisted of convertible bonds, but in 1968 they represented more than half of the greatly increased total of new Euro-bond issues.

The advantages of convertible bonds from the point of view of their holders may be summarised as follows:

(1) They provide a hedge against a considerable erosion of their capital to be caused by a depreciation of their currency. The hedge does not cover a depreciation of the currency that would cause the equities to rise merely to the extent of the

conversion premium. But investors are safeguarded to some extent against a depreciation of the currency that would go beyond that extent. Of course in many instances a rise in individual equities exceeds or falls short of the extent corresponding the decline in the purchasing power of the currency concerned. The safeguard provided by holding equities depends, therefore, on the merits or demerits of individual holdings. Nevertheless, unless the choice of bonds is ill-advised or unlucky, the assumption that they provide in a general way a hedge against the erosion of the currency is correct.

(2) On that assumption it may well be asked why investors should not acquire ordinary shares straightaway instead of acquiring bonds enabling them to acquire equities at a later date at considerably higher prices. The answer is that until the conversion is effected investors will benefit by a much higher yield than the one they would obtain on ordinary shares. The interest on convertible bonds is well above the current yield of the shares into which they are convertible, in some instances several times higher.

(3) As the bonds constitute a prior charge on the profits and assets of the issuing or guaranteeing corporation, investment in them involves less risk than investment in ordinary shares. It safeguards holders, up to a point, against setbacks in the earnings of the corporations which would affect dividends on shares and their Stock Exchange prices. This consideration is particularly important in respect of issues by corporations which have yet to prove their earning capacity.

From the point of view of the borrowing corporations, the issue of convertible bonds has the advantage of being able to borrow at a lower cost than through the issue of straight bonds. So far the Euro-issue market has not been organised for the issue of ordinary shares – even though there have been in 1968 and 1969 a few such issues – so that if American corporations, and also non-American corporations which wish to avail themselves of the capital resources of that market instead of borrowing locally or increasing their equity capital, their choice is between issuing straight bonds or convertible bonds.

During a period of creeping inflation it is obviously easier for borrowers to raise capital by means of issuing convertible bonds, as fixed interest-bearing securities are apt to be unpopular and the terms at which they can be issued have to allow for the likelihood of a future depreciation of the monetary unit. On the other hand, convertible bonds offer investors not only a hedge against inflation but also a chance to participate in the benefits derived by the corporation from future growth. In return for such advantages they are prepared to lend at a considerably lower rate of interest. They are thus able to eat some of their cake and keep at least some of it.

When inflation is proceeding at the rate of 4 to 5 per cent per annum even a $7\frac{1}{2}$ per cent bond has only a yield of between $2\frac{1}{2}$ and $3\frac{1}{2}$ per cent in real terms. This is not very attractive even in the case of borrowers of high standing, and is decidedly unattractive in the case of borrowers of inferior standing. It is quite unacceptable from new firms which have yet to prove their worth. On the other hand, the possibility of hedging against inflation and of benefiting by the future growth of the corporation induces investors to be content with a relatively unattractive fixed real yield. This accounts for the strong demand for convertible bonds issued even for firms whose names are far from being household words. In 1968 most of the issues for well-known corporations were over-applied for. Such was their popularity that members of selling syndicates received heavy applications for them even before their actual terms were announced, for fear that by the time the terms became known the issue would be oversubscribed.

This amazing willingness of investors to accept terms before they are known, and the willingness of banking houses of standing to advise their clients to do so, implies a very high degree of confidence in the integrity and fairness of the issuing groups. It is of course to the latters' interests to negotiate reasonable terms, for if they should be found to be disappointing on repeated occasions most investors would not be willing to risk a repetition of the experience and the issuing houses concerned would lose valuable goodwill.

But the fixing of the conversion premium is one of the most involved and most difficult financial operations. The fixing of the interest and issue price of straight bonds is relatively simple. They are based on the response of subscribers to recent comparable straight bond issues, and on the prevailing yields. But when interest, issue price, conversion premium and conversion time limits of convertible bonds are fixed it is necessary to allow for current yields of equities into which the bonds are convertible, for the borrowing corporation's growth prospects and dividend policies, and for the probable general trend of equities as well as of yields on bonds. Moreover, two borrowing corporations are less easily comparable than, say, two borrowing Governments.

If the current yield on equities of well-established concerns is very low, many investors prefer to secure the higher yield they receive on bonds for some years even at the cost of having to forgo the benefit of an appreciation of the shares between the date at which they acquire the bonds and the date at which they can exercise their option. Of course if the conversion premium is not a fixed figure but increases if the option is exercised at a later date then holders are apt to get the worst of both worlds.

Much depends on the dates between which the option can be exercised. It is of course to the interests of the subscribers that the period between the two dates should be long, so as to have a good opportunity for deciding whether it is worth their while to exercise their option. The advantage of higher interest on the bonds compared with the yield on the equities into which they will become convertible has to be compared with the investment premium both on the assumption that it might become worth while for the investor to exercise his option at the earliest possible moment and on the assumption that he would deem it expedient to delay his decision till the last moment. A view has to be taken about the rate at which equities are likely to rise, and about the risk that they might not rise sufficiently by the date of the conversion time limit to make it worth while to exercise the option.

As a general rule the bonds become convertible within a matter of months after their issue and remain convertible right until their maturity. When the conversion premium is substantial the fixing of an early date for the beginning of the convertibility period constitute no real concession, because the chances are that the market price of equities would not rise to anything like the full extent of the conversion premium in a short time. But if future growth is not fully discounted in the current market price of the shares it provides a considerable financial advantage to be able to convert at an early date, because holders are then placed in a position to take their profits if they expect a rise in their shares to be followed by a relapse. If they regarded the rise as purely temporary they would want to convert their bonds and sell their shares. Such considerations are liable to be based, not only on the prospects of individual borrowing firms, but also on views taken on the prospects of general Stock Exchange trends.

As a general rule the bonds become convertible from an early date. It is the time limit for conversions that varies widely. Longer time limit gives lenders a better chance in instances in which the conversion premium is substantial.

Although the yield of convertible bonds is considerably lower than that of straight bonds, they have gained favour among investors and are likely to continue to gain favour so long as the basic trend of equities is upward. Should that trend turn downward, or should there be widespread expectations of such a change, investors would come to prefer one bird in hand to two in the bush – they would want a higher yield on their bonds, having regard to the reduced chances of an opportunity for exercising their option to convert them into equities. At any rate they would only be prepared to invest in convertible bonds with lower conversion premiums.

Towards the close of 1968 another type of Euro-bond made its appearance – the convertible bond with a detachable warrant. These warrants grant holders an option to buy a certain number of ordinary shares at a fixed price that includes a conversion premium. Holders are at liberty to retain their bonds while selling the warrants, or to retain the warrants until they deem it worth while to exercise their option. This type of security has been familiar in the United States for some time, but in 1968 it was practically an innovation in the Euro-bond market. Should the rising trend in equities continue this type of issue is likely to become popular to a considerable degree.

The question is whether the evolution of the Euro-issue market will proceed further and, in addition to providing facilities for the various types of bond issues, will also provide facilities for an international distribution of foreign share issues. There have always been international issues of shares by leading concerns of international standing, such as the big oil companies. But, as observed earlier in this chapter, so far the Euro-issue market has shown but little inclination to take an interest of less generally-known firms. This does not necessarily mean, however, that its attitude might not change under the influence of persistent optimism about the trend of equity price, and of the low yield on shares of concerns of international standing.

The trend of development would point towards the emergence of an active Euro-share market in case of a substantial all-round devaluation of currencies, or a series of individual devaluations, or of depreciations if the system of floating exchange rates should be adopted. In such circumstances the prospects of a prolonged inflationary boom would increase considerably.

At the same time the need for the United States and other countries to defend their currencies by means of abnormally high interest rates and credit squeeze would subside, and borrowers would only be prepared to offer much lower interest rates on straight bonds and also on convertible bonds. Although they would be able to borrow in either form on more favourable terms, the preference of investors for straight equities might induce many firms to raise their capital in that form.

Should such a situation arise, the existence of a highly developed mechanism for the issue of Euro-bonds and for marketing them subsequently would provide attractive opportunities for extending its functions to include the issue of, and trading in, ordinary shares on an international scale.

Meanwhile convertible bonds are the investors' favourites. The *Federal Reserve Bank Monthly Review* of August 1968 states that 'in every instance convertible issues have been oversubscribed at yields less than 5 per cent. This compared with a yield of over 7 per cent on straight dollar Euro-bonds and with a yield of over 6 per cent on D. mark Euro-bonds. By the beginning of 1969 all yields increased, but the differentials remained substantially unchanged. Convertible bonds were expected to continue in favour in the light of the unpopularity of fixed interest-bearing securities, even though they too came under the influence of the setback in the Euro-bond market in the spring of 1969.

Although the high premium on investment dollars is an obstacle to their use for the acquisition of straight Euro-bonds, in given circumstances they might be used for the acquisition of convertible bonds, if and when the prices of the equities concerned has risen sufficiently to make it appear worth while to acquire such bonds.

The popularity of convertible bonds is indicated by the appearance of a leading Swiss industrial firm as a borrower in the Euro-bond market early in 1969. Although the issue is in terms of dollars, it is convertible into Swiss shares. The formula of convertible bonds is liable to attract many lenders and borrowers and it is likely to assume various forms to conform with diverse and changing requirements.

F

CHAPTER SIXTEEN

Trends of Euro-Bond Prices

THE task of ascertaining the rules governing trends in the Euro-bond market is incomparably more complicated than that of ascertaining the rules of fluctuations in the Euro-currency market. For one thing, as far as the latter is concerned, the question of price trends does not arise. Foreign currency deposits that change hands in the Euro-currency market are short-term deposits repayable in a matter of days, weeks or months. Their market is not like the foreign exchange market or the Stock Exchange where prices are quoted but more like the discount market or money market where interest rates are quoted.

It is true, in addition to considerations of yield, considerations of capital gains or losses on Euro-currency transactions are also liable to arise if the borrowed deposits are converted into a different currency without covering the exchange risk. But such considerations need not form an essential part of Euro-currency transactions the majority of which involve no exchange risk, either because the deposits borrowed are used or re-lent in the same currency or because the exchange risk is covered. On the other hand the acquisition of Euro-bonds does entail exchange risk – and also its corollary, the possibility of gains on an appreciation of their currency – unless they are acquired by residents of the country in whose currency the bonds are issued.

Acquisition of straight bonds obviously entail capital gains or losses as a result of an appreciation or depreciation of the currency of their denomination or of the investors' own currency. Their maturity dates are usually too distant to enable holders to cover the exchange risk – unless they acquire the bonds long after their issue – and in many instances holders are not in a position to know when their bonds will be drawn for redemption.

As far as convertible bonds are concerned, prospects of capital gains on their equity contents, and the possibility of capital losses through a depreciation of the shares after holders have exercised their right to convert their bonds, are liable to assume an importance that transcends considerations of yield or of gains or losses on the bonds contents of convertible bonds. Even the yield of these securities becomes highly uncertain once they are converted into equities. It varies from corporation to corporation.

For the above reasons the Euro-bond market is not subject to general trends to the same extent as the Euro-currency market. The rates of various Euro-currencies are also apt to fluctuate independently of each other and sometimes they move in opposite directions. They are liable to come under the influence of the world trend of interest rates, albeit to a varying degree. But then the same is true for Euro-bonds even if they are issued in various denominations. Nevertheless if we compare the behaviour of quotations of Euro-currencies and Euro-bonds of the same denomination – e.g., Euro-dollars with straight dollar Euro-bonds – the rules affecting the former, complicated as they are, are simplicity itself compared with the rules affecting the latter.

Both in the Euro-currency market and in the Euro-bond market different rates are quoted for different maturities. Where the two markets practically meet is in respect of the quotations of long Euro-dollar rates for five years' deposits and of short dollar Euro-bond rates for bonds maturing in five years.

But while standard rates in the Euro-dollar market for any particular maturity are virtually homogenous, Euro-bond issue terms or yields for the same maturities are widely diverse and are affected by different sets of influences. There are no standard terms or yields in the Euro-bond market compared with the standard Euro-currency rates for deposits lent to first-rate borrowers. At any given moment and for any given maturity all banks of first-class standing can borrow Euro-currencies at identical rates, subject only to such minor discrepancies as are liable to arise even in the best market. On the other hand, the issue terms and subsequent quotations of Euro-bonds issued for first-class borrowers are apt to differ from each other at any given moment, because of different influences affecting the market's ever-changing views taken about individual borrowers. Leading banks which borrow Euro-currencies are considered to be in the same class. But borrowers issuing Euro-bonds – whether Government or Government-guaranteed institutions, international organisations, municipal authorities or industrial concerns – are judged in the market and by the investors according to what they consider to be their respective merits. Their judgement is apt to change according to the outstanding amount of the borrowers' bonds and according to a wide variety of other circumstances.

Even in respect of the length of maturity there is a wider variety in the Euro-bond market than in the Euro-currency market. Deposits dealt with in the market as a matter of routine mature from between 2 days and 12 months, even though it is possible to negotiate deposits of up to 5 years. Euro-bonds transacted in the market as a matter of routine mature mostly between 5 years and 20 years.

The influences affecting the market in straight bonds are to a large degree similar to those affecting foreign bonds issued locally and quoted on local Stock Exchanges. But there is an important difference, due to the international character of Euro-bonds. Although many conventional foreign bonds are also international to some extent, the degree to which they are dealt with internationally is much higher for Euro-bonds. This is partly because the latter are held more internationally, but also owing to the mechanism of the secondary market, described in Chapter 7, through which there is a constant stream of dealings, or at any rate quotations, across national borders. For these reasons, Euro-bonds are affected to a higher degree by monetary and economic tendencies prevailing outside countries whose residents hold them. This difference between conventional foreign bonds and straight Euro-bonds is apt to disappear as a result of the growing practice of dealing also in the former through the mechanism of the secondary market set up primarily for meeting the requirements of dealers and investors in Euro-bonds.

The effect of monetary and economic trends of convertible Euro-bonds is of course quite different from its effect on straight Euro-bonds. When a devaluation or a revaluation of their currency of denomination is widely expected it is liable to affect the two types of Euro-bonds to a different degree and, in given circumstances, even in a different sense. Holders of straight bonds are obviously exposed to a loss through a devaluation or depreciation of the currency concerned, and they stand to gain through its revaluation or appreciation. The extent of their losses or gains tends to be identical in the long run with the degree of the change in the value of the currency concerned, even though we saw earlier that in the case of the materialisation of a widely-anticipated revaluation large-scale profit-taking is liable to reduce the bondholders' immediate profit.

To the extent to which convertible bonds are held for the sake of their fixed yield they are subject to the same influences whenever their currency is devaluation-prone or revaluation-prone, though the degree of such influences is liable to be offset, and more than offset, by the extent to which the bonds are held for the sake of their potential equity-content. A devaluation of the currency of the debtor country is apt to cause an increase in equities in excess of the devaluation and the stage at which it would become worth while for holders to exercise their option is liable to be reached earlier. This would mean that the adverse effect of the devaluation on the interest payments in terms of the bondholders' own currency and, in the event of a realisation of the bonds, on their proceeds, would be of shorter duration.

Whether the favourable effect of a devaluation on the equity content of the Euro-bonds outweighs the unfavourable effect on their bond content depends largely on the magnitude of the conversion premium. In many instances that premium is fixed at such a high figure that the growth prospects of the corporation concerned are discounted in it for a great many years ahead. In that case bondholders must put up with the adverse effect of the devaluation on the bond content of their convertible bonds for a long time before they would have a chance to benefit by the favourable effect on its equity content. If the intervening period is long there is always the risk of circumstances arising in which the investor has to realise his holding at a substantial capital loss. For this reason the prices of bonds with very large conversion premiums might be affected unfavourably by a devaluation even if the growth prospects of the corporation concerned are favourable in the long run.

Revaluation prospects tend to affect the prices of straight bonds favourably. To the extent to which convertible bonds are held for the sake of their bond content – for instance in countries where domestic interest rates are comparatively low – they tend to be affected favourably, unless this effect is offset, and more than offset, by expectations of an adverse effect of a revaluation on growth prospects and therefore on the equity contents of the bonds. The deflationary or disinflationary effect of a revaluation tends to delay growth and to hold back or even reverse the rise in equities on the Stock Exchanges of the debtor countries. This means that the moment when it is likely to become worth while for bondholders to exercise their option would become deferred. But since a revaluation increases the proceeds of interest payments in terms of the bondholders' currency – it might also yield a capital profit if they realise the bonds before it becomes worth while to convert them – they are liable to be compensated and more than compensated for the adverse effect on its equity content.

Inflation prospects tend to cause a depreciation of straight Euro-bonds. Investors have to discount a decline in the purchasing power of interest and principal, in addition to a decline in the market prices of their bond as a result of an increase in long-term interest rates and a diversion of investment funds from bonds into equities as a hedge against inflation. What matters is not so much inflation prospects in the country in whose currency the bonds are payable – unless such prospects make the currency devaluation-prone – as inflation prospects in the holders' own country or in countries where they could sell their holdings. International inflation, such as has been proceeding during the 'sixties, has been responsible for the all-round decline in the prices of straight Euro-bonds, and for the increase in the level of interest rates at which new bonds could be issued. A yield of, say, 7 per cent is more attractive in a country where inflation is creeping at the rate of 3 per cent p.a. than in a country where it is proceeding at the rate of 5 per cent p.a.

The effect of inflation on convertible bonds, in the absence of fears that the currency of the contract might be devalued, is that its bond content tends to depreciate both in money terms and in real terms, while its equity content tends to appreciate in money terms. Here again much depends on the size of the convertibility premium and on the extent to which the market price has discounted the future growth of the debtor corporation.

Deflation prospects in the investors' country tend to cause straight bonds to appreciate. Investors expect an increase in the purchasing power of interest and principal of their investment, in addition to the increase in their market prices caused by a downward trend of interest rates which develops once the deflationary measures have begun to produce their effects. There will also be a flow of funds from equities into bonds. But if deflation proceeds very far it entails the possibility of a revaluation of the investors' currency, which would mean a fall in the market prices of the straight bonds.

The effect on the market prices of straight bonds of deflation in the country in whose currency the bonds are issued is determined by the extent to which such deflation gives rise to expectations of a revaluation of the currency concerned.

Market prices of convertible bonds are affected favourably by deflation in the investing country as far as their bond contents are concerned and remain unaffected as far as their equity contents are concerned. Here again the size of the convertibility premium and the extent to which future growth is discounted in issue terms and in market prices is of considerable importance.

The movements of prices of straight bonds in response to revaluation or devaluation prospects in the lending countries, or in response to deflation or inflation, tend to be sympathetic, subject only to divergencies due to changes in the relative prospects of the borrowers. But we must always bear in mind that a currency may appear to be devaluation-prone in relation to one currency and at the same time stable or even revaluation-prone in relation to some other currency. Owing to the essentially international character of Euro-bonds, there is always a possibility of conflicting cross-currents of buying or selling on the part of various investing countries, resulting from discrepancies between fundamental monetary trends.

The response of prices of convertible bonds to basic monetary changes or expectations of changes is much more complicated. The prices vary widely according to the individual circumstances of borrowing corporations and according to their terms of convertibility. A further complicating element is the ever-changing trend of the local markets concerned. Discrepancies between their trends are bound to develop. Such discrepancies are liable to affect convertible bonds to a much higher degree than straight bonds. But equity markets all over the world are liable to respond more or less to trends in Wall Street. Although Euro-bonds cannot be transacted in Wall Street for U.S. residents the trend of convertible bonds in markets outside the United States is far from indifferent to Wall Street trends. A boom in Wall Street expressing optimism about the prospect of American corporations is liable to increase the attraction of convertible bonds issued by those self-same American corporations in Europe, but to some extent convertible bonds issued by non-American corporations and even those issued in currencies other than the dollar are also liable to be affected.

Trends of equity prices on local Stock Exchanges in the investing countries, too, are apt to influence investors' decisions whether to switch into convertible bonds for the sake of growth prospects the equity contents of the bonds, compared with the growth prospects of local equities. The effect is, of course reciprocal. So is the reaction of various local markets to each others' trends.

If local investors are only permitted to subscribe or buy with the aid of investment currencies the premium on such currencies – provided it is not prohibitive – and expectations of changes in that premium are further complicating factors. Any possible changes in exchange control regulations in respect of portfolio investments, and any changes in the spirit in which the regulations are actually applied, have to be borne in mind as influences liable to affect Euro-bond prices.

We saw in earlier chapters how Euro-currency rates, interest rates and exchange rates tend to affect Euro-bond rates. Broadly speaking, such effects tend to be similar on various kinds of Euro-bonds in terms of the same currency. And in spite of the diversity of considerations and influences dealt with in this chapter, there is such a thing as a basic trend in the Euro-bond market – or at any rate two basic trends in the markets in straight bonds and convertible bonds respectively – even though there are bound to be numerous divergencies from the basic trends. But then, after all, the fact that changes in individual equities in Wall Street are liable to diverge considerably from the Dow Jones index does not invalidate the existence of basic trends broadly indicated by that index. An index of Euro-bond prices is a better indication of the international trend, and even of the inter-European trend, than an index compiled on the basis of trends of equities in European Stock Exchanges, because, owing to the international turnover in the secondary market and the international placing of Euro-bonds, their prices are more likely to respond to international supply-demand relationship.

CHAPTER SEVENTEEN

The Market in Investment Dollars

THE continued existence of the system to be described in this chapter depends on the maintenance of exchange control measures, in so far as they relate to portfolio investments abroad, substantially in their present form. The basic principle of the system of investment currencies is that under its application transactions in foreign securities cannot affect the balance of payments. This at any rate was the position until April 1965 when a provision was introduced under which holders selling investment currencies have to sell 25 per cent of the amount as ordinary currencies, thereby bringing support to the balance of payments on capital account. More will be said about this modification of the operation of the system later in this chapter. Meanwhile we shall confine ourself with the system as it operates without regard to the element of complication introduced by its modification in 1965.

From an American point of view investment dollars differ in no way from ordinary U.S. dollars. Both types are dollars deposited by residents in the United Kingdom with a bank situated in the United States. They are completely indistinguishable from ordinary dollars under United States law or practice. The difference arises from British exchange control regulations. U.K. residents can only use investment dollars for the purchase of dollar securities or of other foreign securities quoted on a recognised foreign Stock Exchange. They have to be declared by authorised dealers or other authorised depositaries, in returns submitted to the Bank of England. Their holders are always entitled to sell them as ordinary dollars – if they were foolish enough to do so – and for this reason investment dollars could never go to a discount in any circumstances. In actual practice they have always been at a premium which rose from time to time to a very high level, precisely because they can be used for the purchase of foreign securities for which purpose ordinary dollars could only be used with special permission that is not granted easily.

Investment dollars, together with non-resident account sterling and property dollars, are the last survivors of the multiple currency system that emerged during and after the war. Although it was suggested from time to time that they should be abolished because their wide premium tends to discredit sterling, up to the time of writing they have been allowed to continue albeit their form underwent from time to time drastic modifications. Until May 1962 there were two categories of investment currencies. They were popularly called 'hard dollars' and 'soft dollars', according to whether they could be used for the purchase of North American securities or of other foreign securities. Today investment dollars – known also as 'security dollars', 'Premium dollars' or 'switch dollars' – can be used for the purchase of any eligible non-sterling securities.

The same rules apply to the proceeds of the sale of foreign securities in terms of currencies other than the dollar. The proceeds of the sale of German securities held by U.K. residents, for instance, are 'investment marks' and can now be used for the purchase of foreign securities in any denomination. For this reason discrepancies between the premium on investment dollars and on other investment currencies, which are in practice completely interchangeable, are limited to the cost of switching into the currency needed for the purchase of bonds which are in terms of a different currency.

Although from time to time the premium on investment dollars was low enough to make it worth while for U.K. residents to use them for acquiring Euro-bonds, at the time of writing it is quoted around 50 per cent. This effectively rules out their use in connection with Euro-bonds. Nevertheless, the inclusion of their description in a book on Euro-bonds is not irrelevant, for situations might arise sooner or later when it would become once more worth while for U.K. residents to subscribe or buy Euro-bonds with the aid of investment dollars. But, having regard also to the loss suffered by sellers as a result of the provision under which 25 per cent of the investment dollars sold by their holders have to be sold as ordinary dollars, the premium would have to decline very considerably before such a situation could even be envisaged.

The market in investment dollars has arisen from exchange control on capital transfers by U.K. residents. The system aims at preventing an unauthorised increase in U.K. portfolio investments abroad, by ensuring that foreign securities can only be acquired out of the proceeds of the sale of foreign securities formerly held by U.K. residents. Originally the same principle was applied to non-resident holdings of British securities. The proceeds of their sales became 'security sterling' which in theory, could only be used – apart from certain exceptions – for the purchase of other British securities. In 1967 security sterling was unified with external account sterling which is convertible by its non-resident holders into foreign currencies. This means that the proceeds of non-resident portfolio investments in Britain are no longer 'blocked'. They can now be withdrawn, but British portfolio investments remain subject to restrictions.

The system of investment dollars came into being in October 1947 when wartime exchange restrictions were relaxed and U.K. residents were authorised for the first time since the war to acquire new holdings of foreign securities – as distinct from turning over their existing foreign portfolio investments – provided they were prepared to pay the premium on investment dollars. Until then U.K. residents were only allowed to buy foreign securities out of the proceeds of the foreign securities they themselves had sold, and the exact proceeds had to be reinvested immediately. This new formula was an important concession, mitigating the rigidity of the system, because under it U.K. residents came to be authorised to reinvest in foreign securities the proceeds of foreign securities sold by other U.K. residents.

The authorities retained a high degree of control over foreign security transactions by making it compulsory for banks and other authorised depositaries for foreign securities – Stock Exchange firms, insurance companies, investment trusts, solicitors, etc. – to declare to the Bank of England within two months each change in their holdings held for the accounts of their clients.

The bulk of business in investment currencies is concluded outside the Stock Exchange. Their market differs in some respects from the market in ordinary foreign exchange. To a large but varying extent business in investment dollars was originally transacted between stock departments of banks and Stock Exchange firms specialising in foreign securities. But as a result of the high proportion of transactions not related directly to security transactions, foreign exchange departments came to take a more active hand in the market. Gradually specialisation was carried a stage further. One dealer, or several dealers in foreign exchange departments came to specialise in investment currencies, and the more active firms set up separate departments which have to keep in close touch both with the foreign exchange department and with the securities department of their banks.

Although there is a large number of authorised dealers, the active market never included more than about two dozen banks, not even before the turnover came to decline as a result of the tightening of rules in 1957. Firms with a large turnover often have an opportunity to 'marry' buying and selling orders of their clients, in which case the transactions circumvent the market. Business is transacted in the market as a rule without the intermediary of foreign exchange brokers. Apart from this, the technique of dealing and the mechanism of the market is similar to that of the foreign exchange market.

Investment dollars can be bought and sold for forward as well as spot delivery. In the absence of provisions to the contrary, spot investment currencies are due to be delivered and paid for two clear days after the conclusion of the deal, the practice being the same as in the foreign exchange market. But owing to the special character of business in investment currencies, whenever a transaction is connected with a security purchase the delivery of the investment dollars is synchronised with the settlement of the security transaction.

Originally this was a relatively simple matter for securities transacted on Stock Exchanges, because deliveries were made on fixed settlement days, and most forward transactions in investment dollars were for those dates. In the meantime, however, as a result of the development of the secondary market in Euro-bonds between banks, a large and increasing proportion of business in foreign securities is transacted outside Stock Exchanges. Moreover, as we saw earlier, long delays came to develop during the late 'sixties in the delivery of Euro-bonds, so that dates of completion became quite uncertain. Buyers of Euro-bonds have no means of knowing for what date they need the investment dollars, and no option market has developed to enable them to buy from their banks forward investment dollars with optional dates of delivery. The usual practice is to instruct their banks to buy spot investment dollars and hold them until they are required.

There was before the changes in exchange regulations in 1965 and 1967 a very active forward market in investment dollars. The technique of the operation is substantially the same as that of ordinary forward exchange operations. When a dealer sells investment dollars for forward delivery – whether to a client outside the market or to another dealer in the market – he immediately covers the exchange risk and the premium risk by buying spot investment dollars. Covering of the exchange risk alone by buying ordinary dollars would not be satisfactory, because the premium usually fluctuates much more widely than the spot rate or the forward rate.

As a result of the purchase of spot investment dollars the dealer has the use of the dollars until the forward contract matures. The same is the situation if, owing to the uncertainty of the delivery date, he buys for his client spot investment dollars and holds them for his client's account. He may lend these dollars in the Euro-dollar market. Or he may carry out an ordinary swap transaction, selling the spot dollars against forward dollars to be delivered when the forward contract in investment dollars matures. If the date when the investment dollars are required is uncertain he may employ the dollars in short swap transactions or in short Euro-dollar transactions, so as to be able to regain their possession at short notice. Or he may rely on his ability to buy or borrow dollars for immediate delivery if called upon to deliver them before his Euro-dollar transaction or his swap transaction matures.

When a dealer buys forward investment dollars – whether from a client or in the market – he immediately sells spot investment dollars out of his holding of such dollars. Dealers are permitted to carry such holdings in order to be able to provide facilities for their customers. In earlier years they were in a position to speculate on a large scale by going long or short in investment dollars, but now they are not supposed to hold larger stocks than is justified by the volume of business with their clients or by reasonable expectations of an increase of that volume. They have to report their holdings to the Bank of England and if the latter should consider the holdings of a bank in excess of legitimate requirements that bank is called upon to reduce its holdings. In any case, the fact that investment dollars are taken into account for the purpose of the limits for foreign exchange commitments fixed by the authorities for each bank tends to discourage excessive holdings.

As a result of the official discouragement of speculation in investment dollars, on top of the discouraging effect of the rule under which 25 per cent of the investment dollars sold by their clients has to be sold as ordinary dollars, the turnover in investment dollars was in the late 'sixties much smaller than it had been some years earlier. Consequently, the number of houses dealing actively in the market has become reduced to some half dozen. In any case, it was a risky market owing to the wide fluctuations of the premium. Unlike pre-war dealers, operators in foreign exchanges under the Bretton Woods system of narrow fluctuations between support points were not used to unlimited fluctuations. Whenever they came to be caught badly by an unexpected sharp rise or fall in the premium their banks decided to withdraw from active dealing and to confine activities to covering transactions with their clients. Hence the gradual reduction in the number of active dealers.

The charge to customers on forward transactions in investment dollars is usually based on the swap rates on ordinary dollars and on the premium on investment dollars. But, as remarked above, the uncertainty of delivery dates has made it necessary to cover a high proportion of customers' requirements by purchases of spot investment dollars.

Firms actively dealing in investment dollars are prepared to make two-way quotations with a relatively narrow margin between buying and selling rates. Possibly in the majority of instances they make two-way quotations, not because it is a matter of indifference for them which way they deal at the prices quoted, but solely in order not to disclose their intention. This is all the more important as they do not use foreign exchange brokers as intermediaries. If a bank quotes investment dollars at a premium of, say, $50\frac{1}{4}$ to $50\frac{1}{2}$ it may only want to buy at $50\frac{1}{4}$ or to sell at $50\frac{1}{2}$, but once the rates are quoted and accepted immediately it may have to engage in a transaction in the unwanted sense, even though he may only buy or sell the minimum amount customary in such operations.

Technically it is possible to conclude forward business up to six months. Owing to the rule under which holders other than dealers have to surrender another 25 per cent as ordinary dollars after six months there is no business for longer periods.

In theory the maximum of the supply of investment dollars is represented by the total market value of dollar securities held by residents in the U.K. According to the Radcliffe Report, the size of this 'dollar pool' out of which the supply of investment dollars can be increased was estimated to be of the order of $4,000 million in 1959 at prevailing market prices. Giving evidence before the Radcliffe Committee for the Treasury, Sir Dennis Rickett stated that this amount tended to increase as a result of gaps in exchange control. Owing to the inadequacy in certain parts of the Sterling Area such as the countries of the Persian Gulf or Hong Kong, additional dollar securities had been brought 'to inside the ring fence'. That gap was said to have been closed in July 1957, since when U.K. residents are no longer supposed to be able to acquire foreign securities from other countries of the Sterling Area. Even so, the control is not altogether watertight.

In any case there are various other channels through which the 'pool' can be increased legitimately. Most important amongst them is the increase in the market value of dollar securities and other foreign securities. At the end of 1967, after the devaluation of sterling, the value of U.K. holdings of dollar securities was officially estimated at £5,640 million. This in spite of the reduction of this pool through the operation of the rule under which 25 per cent of the investment currencies sold by holders other than authorised dealers have to be sold as ordinary dollars. Between April 1965 and August 1968 U.K. residents' ability to buy and hold dollar securities was reduced by that device by some $750 million.

There may be additions to the 'pool' through receipts of legacies or gifts from abroad, through the addition of immigrants' holdings, realisations of various assets abroad by U.K. residents, life endowment policies abroad, etc. On the other hand, the 'pool' is reduced through exports of securities by emigrants and repatriations by non-residents etc. But, as pointed out above, the most important means of reducing the 'pool' is through compulsory sales of investment dollars as ordinary dollars. As only 75 per cent of the amounts of the proceeds of foreign securities reaches the investment dollar market, so much less is available for those wanting to buy foreign securities.

The officially endorsed idea that the total of private holdings of dollar securities constitutes the potential supply of investment dollars is open to criticism. In the same sense it would be justified to contend that, in the absence of exchange restrictions, the gigantic total of banks deposits and note issue in the United Kingdom, plus the Stock Exchange value of all sterling securities, constitutes the 'sterling pool' representing the maximum amount of sterling that could be sold in the foreign exchange market. In reality only a small fraction of that total is ever offered or is available for sale in the foreign exchange market. Similarly, only a fraction of the dollar securities and other foreign securities is ever likely to be made available at any given moment, or even over a given period, to satisfy the demand for investment dollars. Most of these securities are held firmly by institutions or by private investors. While in theory it is conceivable that a very sharp rise in the prices of the securities and/or a very sharp rise in the premium on investment dollars might induce many of them to sell their securities, the 25 per cent rule tends to discourage holders of securities from realising their holdings.

There is of course a certain amount of liquid investment dollars held by investors who intend to reinvest their capital sooner or later. But the approach of the time limit of 6 months after which 50 per cent would have to be sold as ordinary dollars, and even more of the time limit of 12 months after which the whole amount would have to be so sold, might force holders to sell them in a hurry, even at a relatively unfavourable rate. Even if they only have to surrender 25 per cent, they stand to lose unless they had been lucky enough to have bought their investment dollars at a much lower premium. Thus with the premium at, say, 48, they avoid a loss if they had bought their investment dollars at a premium of 36 per cent or less.

Between them the 25 per cent rule and the limitation of holdings by dealers tend to discourage speculation in investment dollars. But it is very much a matter of opinion whether the policy aimed at a drastic curtailment of speculation has been advantageous on balance. In the absence of active speculation even a moderate buying or selling by investors is liable to cause a disproportionately sharp rise or fall in the premium, because a counterpart is not readily forthcoming.

A controversial question is if, and to what extent, the 25 per cent rule has been responsible for the sharp rise in the premium. It is true, the immediate effect of the adoption of the rule in 1965 was a doubling of the premium. But its rise from 9 to 20 per cent may be explained by the fact that after the advent of the Labour Government it was widely expected that holders might be compelled to surrender their entire holdings as ordinary dollars, so that the actual measure adopted in April 1965 was received with some relief. More will be said about the effects of exchange controls or of expectations of exchange controls later in this chapter.

It is highly questionable whether a deliberate policy aimed at widening the premium was wise. It certainly tends to produce an adverse psychological effect on sterling.

The rules that govern movements of the premium differ in many respects from those affecting ordinary exchange rate movements. Conventional foreign exchange theory is often unable to explain or forecast the ups and downs of the premium. While occasionally the premium moves in sympathy with spot dollars and with forward rates, more often than not it is largely, and at times completely, independent of them.

Our next step is to examine systematically the influences affecting the movements of the premium on investment currencies. In order to simplify the analysis we propose to confine ourselves to movements of investment dollars.

The following are the circumstances in which the premium on investment dollars tends to rise:

(1) If earnings on dollar equities or on dollar bonds are expected to rise.

(2) If Wall Street is firm or is expected to be firm for any other reason.

(3) If the dollar's prospects are viewed favourably.

(4) If U.K. residents holding dollar securities who had safeguarded themselves against a fall in the premium on investment dollars no longer deem it necessary to maintain the hedge.

(5) If U.S. taxation on corporation profits or on interest on bonds is reduced or is expected to be reduced.

(6) If earnings on British equities or bonds fall or are expected to fall.

(7) If prices on the London Stock Exchange decline or are expected to decline for any other reasons.

(8) If sterling's prospects are regarded as unfavourable.

(9) If there is an increase in hedging against anti-capitalist measures in Britain.

(10) If certain British taxation is increased or is expected to be increased.

(11) If large amounts of new dollar issues are made or are expected to be made in Europe.

(12) If additional permits are issued, or are expected to be issued, for the use of investment dollars for direct investment abroad.

(13) If other kinds of demand for dollars are diverted into the investment dollar market by official measures.

(14) If exchange control relating to capital exports is tightened without, however, affecting the continued existence of the investment dollar system.

(15) If dealers' holdings of investment dollars are low.

(16) If the volume of capital available for investing in dollar securities is increased.

(17) If there is much call option dealing in dollar securities and if many buyers of options deem it necessary to cover by forward purchases of investment dollars.

(18) If for no matter what reason dealers and investors rightly or wrongly expect a widening of the premium.

Whenever dollar securities become more attractive to British residents the resulting demand tends to cause a rise in the premium on investment dollars. British holders are more reluctant to sell unless the sterling price of dollar securities or the premium on investment dollars rises to a level at which they become tempted to take their profits. We saw above that, if demand exceeds the supply held by dealers, would-be buyers have to bid up the premium in order to induce dealers to create additional investment dollars by selling dollar securities, or to induce investors to sell investment dollars they hold in readiness for future investment, or even to induce investors to sell securities in order to benefit by the high premium. An anticipation of an increase in the demand for dollar securities, whether because of favourable earnings prospects or of a cut, or even an expectation of a cut, of the U.S. tax on corporation profits, or for no matter what other reason, tends to put up the premium even before the actual pressure of additional demand for investment dollars becomes evident.

A similar effect is produced if the demand or anticipated demand for dollar securities is due not to an anticipation of their appreciation but to an anticipation of a fall in sterling securities, whether through a decline or anticipated decline in corporation earnings in Britain, or an increase in their taxation, or through no matter what other reason. Even if dollar securities do not become more attractive in an absolute sense, they become more attractive in a relative sense, which is sufficient reason for investors to acquire investment dollars.

Buyers and holders of dollar securities, having safeguarded themselves against the risk of a decline in the premium by selling investment dollars forward, may change their view about the prospects of the premium in which case they cover their short position and this causes an appreciation of investment dollars.

The Treasury's decisions to grant permits for the use of investment dollars by industrial firms for direct investment abroad were mainly responsible for the sharp rise in the premium in recent years. Even anticipation of the granting of additional permits for impending major projects was sufficient to cause a rise in the premium. Rumours about impending permits affected the premium from time to time. In the prolonged absence of any confirmation of such rumours it tended to drift back towards its previous level though not necessarily to the full extent. Diversion of substantial amounts of investment dollars from the market for financing direct investment reduced the supply available for its normal use. Diversion of additional supplies to finance purchases of property abroad produced a similar effect, until the adoption of the system of property dollars the premium on which was for a long time even higher than the premium on investment dollars. But in 1968 the situation became reversed, because uncertainty about political prospects in France and rising cost of upkeep induced many U.K. residents owning villas in the South of France to dispose of their property.

The premium on investment dollars owes its very existence to the maintenance and efficient enforcement of exchange control on the export of capital. It would not have risen to well above 50 per cent in 1968 if U.K. residents found it comparatively easy and safe to circumvent exchange restrictions in preference to paying such high premium. It was because the system of foreign-owned blocked security sterling was leaking like a sieve that the discount on that type of sterling was always comparatively negligible until security sterling was abolished in 1967 through unifying it with external account sterling. But British people are on the whole law-abiding, which means that the premium would have to rise even higher before many of the least scrupulous amongst them yielded to the temptation of breaking the law instead of paying the high premium. If major loopholes were discovered through which it would be possible to circumvent the control with comparative safety it would lower the premium to a level at which most people would no longer deem it worth their while to break the law. On the other hand, a tightening of the control tends to bring the premium to a level at which the less scrupulous section of the financial community deems it worth while to risk resorting to unlawful action – unless the increased risk of being found out or the increased penalties deter them from yielding to the increased temptation.

But if the anticipated exchange control measures are such as to give rise to fears about the seller's ability to deliver the investment dollars, or if the possibility of a compulsory surrender of investment dollars as ordinary dollars is envisaged, the effect is a decline in the demand for investment dollars and a fall of its premium. As pointed out above, this was actually what happened towards the end of 1964 and early 1965, following on the advent of the Labour Government. When it was found that in this respect at any rate the Government's bark was worse than its bite the premium recovered.

If for no matter what reason an increase in the premium is anticipated, the demand for investment increases because investors and speculators want to make a profit on their increase.

Before 1967 the wide fluctuations in investment dollars attracted a large volume of speculative activity to the market. Although the fluctuations have become even wider since the tightening of regulations there is now much less speculation.

The persistently high level of the premium may appear to offer temptation for going short in investment dollars, but in existing circumstances that is not so easy as it was in earlier years. Besides, those who did go short on various occasions since the devaluation in 1967 were so often disappointed as a result of further rises of the premium to new record levels that the possibility of its further rise is widely considered to be well on the cards even when the rate is above 50 per cent.

The following is a summary of the effects produced by a rise in the premium:

(1) Quotations of dollar equities in terms of sterling tend to rise in sympathy with the rise in the premium, allowing for the loss of the premium on 25 per cent of the amount.

(2) The resulting reduction in the sterling yield on dollar securities changes the differential between their yield and that of comparable sterling securities in favour of the latter, thereby tending to divert demand to sterling securities.

(3) A high premium, in the absence of expectations of its further rise, tends therefore to discourage demand for dollar equities, unless a further rise in Wall Street is anticipated.

(4) In the absence of expectations of a further rise in the premium or in Wall Street an increase in the premium tends to cause profit-taking by holders of dollar securities.

(5) Although an increase in the premium has no direct bearing on the balance of payments, it tends to affect sterling unfavourably because it is regarded as an indication weakening confidence in sterling.

(6) As already pointed out, a wider premium tends to stimulate evasion of exchange control.

The ups and downs of the premium are apt to be even more

perplexing than those of exchange rates. On many occasions in recent years even specialists were completely mystified by some unexpected declines in the premium. Such declines are liable to occur in the following circumstances:

(1) If U.S. corporation earnings fall, or are expected to fall.

(2) If dollar equities are expected to fall for any other reasons.

(3) If the prospects of the dollar are expected to be unfavourable.

(4) If U.K. buyers or holders of dollar securities decide to cover the premium risk by selling investment dollars forward.

(5) If the U.S. corporation profits tax increases or is expected to increase.

(6) If the capital gains tax is expected to increase.

(7) If earnings on British equities increase or are expected to increase.

(8) If British equities are expected to appreciate for any other reasons.

(8) If hedges previously arranged against the adoption of anti-capitalist measures are removed.

(9) If British taxation on corporation profits is reduced or is expected to be reduced.

(10) If sterling's prospects are viewed with optimism.

(11) If there is a decline in the use of investment dollars for direct investment.

(12) If permits are granted for financing portfolio investments with the aid of borrowed dollars instead of investment dollars.

(13) If exchange control relating to capital exports is relaxed or if it comes to be evaded more extensively.

(14) If a ban on dealings in investment dollars or a commandeering of dollar securities by the Government is anticipated.

(15) If holdings of investment dollars by dealers or by their clients are large.

(16) If the amount of capital available for investment in dollar securities declines.

(17) If for no matter what other reason a fall in the premium is rightly or wrongly anticipated.

A diversion of demand for portfolio investment from the investment dollar market occurs when the authorities authorise certain investors or financial houses to pay for dollar securities with the aid of dollars borrowed in the United States, or with the aid of Euro-dollars. Occasionally even the temporary use of ordinary dollar holdings is permitted for approved portfolio investment, to avoid the development of a stringent situation.

It is necesasry to deal with the paradoxical situation that is liable to arise when the premium is wide and is not expected to rise further. Although further demands for dollar securities means an additional demand for investment dollars by buyers, this demand does not cause the premium to widen, because its effect is offset by forward selling of investment dollars by the buyers of dollar securities who wish to hedge against a fall in the premium.

Although there is no justification for regarding the investment dollar premium as a barometer indicating the extent of an overvaluation of sterling, to some extent the premium does express in certain circumstances market opinion on the prospects of the sterling-dollar rate. On various occasions when sterling came under a cloud during the post-war period the premium was inclined to widen. This was because to some extent investment dollars or dollar securities bought with the aid of investment dollars were used as a hedge against devaluation. But on other occasions pressure on sterling was not accompanied by a widening of the premium on investment dollars.

The experience of 1949 conclusively proved that the use of investment dollars, or the purchase of dollar securities as a hedge against devaluation was ill-advised, because the premium had already discounted the devaluation. On the eve of the devaluation of sterling the premium on investment dollars was 36 per cent, and immediately after the devaluation it went down to 4 per cent. Considering that the extent of the devaluation was 30½ per cent, those who bought investment dollars as a hedge on the eve of the devaluation lost on the fall of the premium more than they gained on the rise in the sterling-dollar rate. Although the extent to which the prices of individual dollar securities was affected by the devaluation varied widely, in the majority of instances the rise in their sterling price did not fully compensate holders for the fall in the premium. That is to say, if they sold out immediately after the devaluation they suffered a loss, but if they waited a little longer the premium rose once more, and it soon reached at which they were able to realise their holdings at a profit. Even so the experience of 1949 goes to show that the insurance premium against devaluation represented by the premium on investment dollars on the eve of devaluations is apt to be grossly excessive. That experience repeated itself after the devaluation of 1967, although the resulting drop in the premium was of very brief duration.

It is, of course, much cheaper to insure against devaluation by means of forward exchange operations. During the first half of 1967 the covering of the exchange risk by means of forward selling of sterling cost much less than 1 per cent, while the premium on investment dollars was fluctuating between 20 and 25 per cent. The difference is even more striking than would appear from these figures if we remember that for brief periods the actual cost of forward cover was a bare fraction per annum, while the cost of covering by buying investment dollars is the same for a day as for a year. But U.K. residents can only use forward exchange facilities if they are engaged in foreign trade or in other approved international transactions. Otherwise the only legitimate channel through which they could attempt to insure themselves against the effects of a devaluation of sterling would be by buying investment dollars. With the premium at its present level, and owing to the provision under which they would have to sell 25 per cent as ordinary dollars, it would take an overdose of optimism about the future of the premium to engage in such an operation.

Political prospects are a much more important long-term

factor in determining the premium. During 1963–64 its high level was largely due to fears of a Socialist victory at the approaching general election, fears which induced many investors to switch into dollar securities. The premium declined below 10 per cent in August 1964 when Conservative prospects appeared to improve. Later the premium widened once more, but contrary to expectations it narrowed considerably after the much-feared Socialist victory. As already pointed out, this was because it was expected that the Labour Government would compel the surrender of investment dollars at ordinary dollar rates.

War scares tend to widen the premium because, although modern wars are apt to be world-wide, it is assumed by many U.K. residents that their capital would be safer if invested across the Atlantic, even though American industries would be within the range of inter-continental rockets.

We already pointed out that over a period of years the authorities in Holland and Belgium intervened systematically in order to keep the premium on the types of currencies corresponding to the British investment dollars at a very low level. They were under no obligation to do so and could at any time discontinue their support. The Belgian authorities actually did so during the troubled period that followed the granting of independence to the Congo, when the premium rose to a high level for a short time.

The British official policy is against intervention to prevent a widening of the premium, even though measures are adopted from time to time which tend to lower it or at any rate check its rise. Only on one isolated occasion, in 1964, were there indications of official support, to prevent a spectacular widening of the premium in connection with the general election. The diversion of demand by property purchasers abroad tended to keep the premium lower, but the granting of licenses for the purpose of acquiring direct investments abroad produced the opposite effect. On balance the object or incidental effects of measures adopted since the advent of the Labour Government tended to widen the premium.

If this is the result of a deliberate policy and not of incompetent handling of a difficult technical problem it shows a singular lack of judgement. For under the existing system there is no point in trying to discourage the buying of American or other foreign securities by U.K. residents. They can only increase their holdings if other U.K. residents reduce theirs, so that operations with the aid of investment dollars could not increase the export of U.K. capital. On the contrary, under the 25 per cent arrangements each time foreign securities change hands within the U.K. the total of U.K. holdings is reduced by 25 per cent. The psychological effect of an unduly wide premium is adverse to sterling, and it is utterly futile to try to persuade public opinion and market opinion that the premium is no true indication of the weakness of sterling. So long as that opinion is held widely at home and abroad, its effect on sterling cannot be ignored. In any case, as pointed out above, unduly high premium increases the temptation to find loopholes in the exchange control through which to export capital.

An argument in favour of the official policy is that the Government prefers direct investment abroad to portfolio investment abroad, and it wishes to tolerate the former without adding to the adverse effect of capital exports on the balance of payments. Possibly the authorities have become misled by their own estimate of the size of the 'dollar pool'. On the assumption that thousands of millions of dollars are liable to be thrown on the market it might appear expedient to reduce the extent of that potential selling pressure. But on any assumption it seemed absurd to encourage wealthy British people to establish residence abroad by making it easier for them to buy the necessary foreign exchange on the property dollar market at a lower premium rather than compel them to pay the high premium prevailing in the investment dollar market.

What determines the demand for investment dollars and the trend of the premium is first and foremost the view taken in the market and by investors of the prospects of demand for foreign securities and for investment dollars. If the premium widens it is liable to offset the loss of sellers under the 25 per cent rule. But the moment a relapse comes to be widely anticipated it would result in heavy selling of foreign securities and of investment dollars. This means that holders of foreign securities are exposed to losses both on the swings and on the roundabouts. The operation of the 25 per cent rule is bound to exaggerate the extent of such losses and adds, therefore, another element of instability to the influences that tend to affect the market.

CHAPTER EIGHTEEN

Some Broader Implications

WE have already examined several of the broader implications of Euro-bond issues in the chapters on their impact on domestic interest rates, international interest rates, exchange rates and Euro-dollars. Some of these implications call, however, for further considerations, and there are, moreover, additional broader aspects to be considered. To some of them passing reference has already been made but they deserve further attention. The following is a selection of these points, to be covered in the present chapter:

(1) Euro-bond issues, by mobilising dormant holdings of dollars or other hard currencies, contribute towards the increase of international liquidity.

(2) They consolidate dollar balances available for speculation, thereby contributing towards international stability.

(3) In normal conditions they offset adverse balances of payments on current account and neutralise the effect of disequilibrating short-term capital movements.

(4) In abnormal conditions they accentuate the disequilibrium in the balance of payments.

(5) They diffuse capital issuing activity that was centred too one-sidedly in New York until 1963.

(6) They contribute towards a more even international allocation of capital resources.

(7) They contribute towards an integration of the European capital markets.

(8) They further the trend towards an internationalisation of finance.

(9) They strengthen the dollar's rôle as an international

currency by providing it with an important additional international function.

(10) They provide means for reducing discrepancies between long-term and short-term interest rates.

(11) They create a structure of international long-term interest rates towards which local long-term interest rates tend to adjust themselves.

(12) They provide an opportunity for surplus countries to re-lend their surpluses to deficit countries, thereby mitigating international disequilibrium.

One of the many unanswered and possibly unanswerable questions raised by the system of Euro-bond issues is whether its net effect is a mobilisation of dormant dollar balances or a consolidation of fluid balances. Evidently the system produces effects in both senses, so that the question we should like to answer is, which of its two conflicting effects outweighs the other. The answer depends on the kinds of dollar balances used for acquiring the Euro-bonds and also on the intentions of their old owners and their new owners. This subject has already been touched upon in Chapters 9 and 10 when dealing with the impact of Euro-bond issues on Euro-dollars and on the dollar exchange. Owing to its importance it is necessary, however, to examine it more closely. In doing so we must guard ourselves against allowing our conclusions to be influenced by our attitude in favour or against international expansion – whether, in our opinion, a further increase of international liquidity is a Good Thing or a Bad Thing.

European dollar bond issues tend to convert dormant non-resident dollar balances into active non-resident dollars in the following circumstances:

(1) If long-term time deposits or other dormant non-resident balances in the United States, or long-term Euro-dollar deposits, are employed for financing the transactions.

(2) If proceeds of non-residents' dollar securities sold to U.S. residents are used for that purpose.

(3) If the borrower spends the formerly dormant dollars on additional imports of non-American goods.

(4) If the borrower sells formerly dormant dollars in the foreign exchange market and the buyer spends them on additional imports of non-American goods.

(5) If the borrower sells formerly dormant dollars to his monetary authorities and the latter use them on Government expenditure abroad or sell them in support of the local currency, or use them as a basis of domestic credit expansion.

Issues of Euro-bonds tend to consolidate fluid foreign dollar assets in the following circumstances:

(1) If sight deposits or short-term foreign deposits in the U.S., or sight or short-term Euro-dollar deposits or short-term credits are used for financing the investment in dollar bonds.

(2) If subscribers buy dollars formerly held in liquid form.

(3) If the borrower uses the dollar proceeds for the repayment of short-term dollar debts.

(4) If the borrower uses the dollar proceeds to obviate the need for short-term borrowing of dollars.

(5) If the dollars bought from the borrower by his monetary authorities are retained by the latter in the form of dollar reserve without expanding credit, or if they are withdrawn in the form of gold.

Any loosening of dormant dollars furthers the cause of expansion but weakens the cause of stability. Any consolidation of fluid dollars is an advantage from the point of view of stability but a disadvantage from the point of view of expansion. However, to answer the broad question whether loosening or consolidation in general is on balance an advantage or a disadvantage is outside the scope of this book. Our present task is confined to trying to ascertain in which direction the system tends to operate in various conceivable circumstances, without trying to suggest an answer whether its operation is for good or for evil from that point of view. There can be no categorical answer to our question. In any case, the answer has become modified by the Euro-bond market's new rôle – that of providing opportunities for American long-term borrowing abroad.

Another major question is whether the system tends to balance or unbalance the balance of payments. It is understood of course that technically the balance of payments must always balance. What matters is the way in which it balances, in which sense unilateral buying or selling pressure on the exchange through a surplus or a deficit tends to cause exchange movements in order to set in motion the market mechanism to attract counterparts in the form of balancing or disturbing short-term fund movements.

While opinion must be divided about the relative advantages and disadvantages of an increase or reduction of the proportion of fluid and consolidated dollar holdings, there is no room for two opinions on the advantages of equilibrium in the balance of payments – in the sense in which it is achieved without unwanted short-term movements of funds or other unwanted changes in the balance of international indebtedness – even if there is room for disagreement on its place in one's list of priorities.

It is true, a too rigid application of the principle that it is an absolute advantage to keep international accounts in permanent equlibrium would mean a rigid maintenance of the *status quo* in respect of the international distribution of monetary gold reserves. Surpluses and deficits are sometimes necessary in order to bring about a more convenient redistribution of monetary gold. Broadly speaking, however, it remains true that in the interest of international stability it is an advantage if long-term capital movements tend to offset surpluses and deficits on the current balance of payments and on the balance of international movements of short-term funds.

Dollar bond issues in Europe tend to be equilibrating in the following ways:

(1) By diverting borrowing by financially strong countries from New York to their own capital markets.

(2) By diverting borrowing by financially weak countries from New York to financially strong European countries with export surpluses available for the purpose.

(3) By mopping up floating dollars that are liable to cause

G

disequilibrating movements of short-term funds through speculative selling, movement of flight money or arbitrage.

(4) By consolidating foreign short-term debts owed by the United States.

(5) By enabling deficit countries to borrow more than they could have borrowed in the New York market.

(6) By enabling surplus countries to re-lend part of their surpluses.

As in respect of 'fluidity *v.* consolidation', the operation of the system is liable to cut both ways also in respect of its effect on the balance of payments. In the latter respect, however, we are reasonably safe in concluding that by and large it operates in an equilibrating sense. It tends to reduce and even prevent the flagrantly disequilibrating process that was in operation until the middle of 1963, under which surplus countries such as France borrowed in New York in spite of their export surpluses and in spite of their large adverse balance of the United States.

From this point of view international bankers engaged in the Euro-issue market have succeeded where their Governments and Central Banks failed up to the time of writing. It may take years before Special Drawing rights will operate on a sufficiently large scale to become an important factor. The scheme of 're-cycling' of unwanted influx of capital has yet to prove its worth. But the end these proposals aimed at was attained to a by no means negligible degree through the equilibrating effect of Euro-issuing activity on a large-scale. The American trade deficit on current account in 1968 was balanced, not by any official measures aimed at producing additional reserves out of thin air, but by practical operations undertaken by bankers, as a result of which the extent to which Germany re-lent her persistent export surplus was increased considerably in 1968, and so was the extent to which the United States covered her deficit by long-term borrowing.

Progress towards consolidation was also made in 1968 as a result of increased issues of Euro-bonds in terms of D. marks.

In addition to contributing towards the export of Germany's surplus, it provided a channel for converting speculative short-term balances into long-term loans.

Another of the broader implications of the Euro-bond issues is the rôle they play in the diffusion of capital issuing activities which had been centred too one-sidedly in New York until the middle of 1963. Perverted 'uphill' flows of capital, such as the flow from the United States to France referred to in earlier chapters, at a time when the adverse American balance and the favourable French balance called for a flow in the opposite sense, were largely due to the inadequacy of most European capital markets, especially that of Paris. This subject is covered in great detail in the Report of the United States Treasury on *Certain European Capital Markets* and we need not go into it in detail. The reason for the one-sided part played by New York in respect of foreign capital issues after the war was the fact that European financial centres with pre-war traditions for serving as international capital markets had been prevented, by a variety of circumstances, from resuming those functions after the war. Those circumstances were described in great detail in the United States Treasury's Report.

Although it had been for a long time an American ambition that New York should take London's place as the dominant financial centre of the world, the achievement of that ambition in the post-war era was looked upon with mixed feelings in the United States. In more recent years American official circles, political circles and expert opinion have come to realise the grave responsibilities and disadvantages that a quasi-monopolistic position as the world's banker entails. The decision to adopt the Interest Equalisation Tax was the result of this change of attitude in favour of a diffusion of international capital issuing activities, change which came to be expressed by the publication of the United States Treasury's Report published with the declared object of assisting Europe in the development of rival capital markets that would divert business from New York.

A more even international allocation of capital resources is an undisputed advantage from the point of view of international economic progress. From this point of view Euro-bond issues tend to perform the same valuable service in respect of long-term capital as is performed by the Euro-dollar market in the sphere of short-term capital. So long as the perennial adverse balance of payments of the United States continues, the New York capital market is not in a position to meet in full the increased international demand on its resources for long-term capital without accentuating the gravity of the dollar problem. The spectacular increase of foreign long-term borrowing in New York during the first half of 1963 constituted a warning which was wisely heeded by the Washington Administration.

Large-scale issuing of Euro-bonds furthers the cause of a more even allocation of capital resources in the following ways:

(1) They replace the flow of funds from the United States at a time when she has a balance of payments deficit, and they stimulate the outflow of capital from countries, such as Germany, which have balance of payments surpluses.

(2) Conceivably European capital markets supply credit-worthy countries with capital in excess of the amounts they would have been able to raise in New York in the absence of the Interest Equalisation Tax.

(3) In some financial centres Euro-bond issues, by improving the capital market mechanism and by reviving the investors' habit to subscribe to bond issues, tend to revive local capital issuing activities.

(4) Euro-bond issues have internationalised the formerly local character of capital markets that developed in some Continental centres since the war.

The effect of Euro-bond issues on the international distribution of capital is, however, necessarily limited in prevailing circumstances. The new capital markets do not cater for the requirements of developing countries which unfortunately do not enjoy a sufficient degree of confidence to enable them to borrow commercially on mutually acceptable terms, indeed on any terms at all. Bankers responsible for the operation of the Euro-issue market are often criticised by politicians for reserving the facilities of the market for the benefit of advanced or relatively advanced countries. What the critics overlook is that banks are unable to undertake issuing a loan unless they have reason to expect that they are able to find investors willing to acquire and hold the bonds. Few if any investors are prepared in existing circumstances to risk their capital by lending it to countries which are not sufficiently stable politically, economically and financially to be considered creditworthy.

In order to become eligible for borrowing in the Euro-bond market or for that matter in the New York market, the developing countries will have to make considerable progress towards consolidation. In due course their progress may reach a stage at which various issuing groups will compete for their loans. The fact that the granting of long-term foreign loans is no longer a monopoly of the United States should provide some degree of incentive to them to try to qualify for being able to borrow on commercial terms, as sooner or later the existence of rival markets will make their task easier.

Integration of European capital markets was one of the declared aims of the Rome Treaty. So far progress in that direction has been very slow. The barriers between the Six have remained as far as the issuing of foreign loans is concerned. Until 1963 foreign issuing activity consisted mainly of loans issued and placed largely in Germany, Switzerland, Holland and, to a less extent, Britain. It was not until the resumption of London's activity as a centre for issuing foreign loans that foreign loans came to be issued on a European scale and perceptible progress came to be made towards integration of European capital markets, not within the EEC but within the whole of Western Europe including Britain and Switzerland. Dollar issues are still more suitable for transactions of a truly international character than D. mark issues, Swiss franc issues, or even composite unit of account issues.

In an article in the June 1963 *Lloyds Bank Review*, Peter Kenen rightly points out that the weakness of European capital markets could only be remedied if those markets were consolidated. 'They would be more receptive to new issues if one

could buy or sell a European bond on any European market.'
In the post-war world none of the European markets is by itself
in a position to serve as an alternative to the New York bond
market. But an integration of the capital issuing facilities of
all Western European markets has created a foreign bond
market that bears comparison with that of the United States.
It would be idle to speculate what would have happened
if Britain had joined the Common Market. But even without
doing so, the co-operation of London's issuing houses with
those of the Continent has in fact given rise to some degree of
association between the leading non-American capital markets.
It is true, there are still many bond issues made in Germany
and Switzerland in which London banks take no direct part,
and many essentially international loans are issued by syndicates
headed by Continental banks. But since the revival of foreign
bond issuing activity in London a good many truly international
loans have been issued by groups headed by London banks,
despite American participation.

In my article in the June 1964 issue of *The National Banking
Review*, published by the United States Treasury, in which I
reviewed that Treasury's Report on *Certain European Capital
Markets*, I expressed the opinion that the reason why the official
American opinion is now in favour of a diffusion of international
issuing activity was, in addition to a desire to relieve the
American balance of payments, to make more effective the
application of the new monetary policy which aims at influencing the entire structure of interest rates. I already observed that
so long as New York was practically the only capital market in
which countries in need of foreign long-term capital could
borrow on a large scale, any American policy decision to discourage such borrowing by raising long-term interest rates was
doomed to remain largely ineffective. Countries in urgent need
of foreign capital would simply pay the higher interest rates,
especially if even those rates are lower than those obtainable
in their domestic capital markets, and even more if the capital
is unobtainable in their domestic markets.

This means that in the absence of alternative capital markets where long-term loans could be issued on terms comparable with those obtainable in New York, pressure on the dollar due to overlending abroad would remain a perennial influence in spite of high long-term interest rates in New York maintained under the post-Radcliffe monetary policy. The effects of that policy, aimed at mitigating the extent to which domestic short-term borrowers have to be penalised under the orthodox monetary policy by shifting part of the burden on long-term borrowers, would be largely frustrated unless a diffusion of international capital issuing activity made that policy more effective.

There is of course room for two opinions whether the new monetary policy is on balance advantageous. Since its object is to maintain business expansion in the United States at an unduly high rate, its advantages in the short run had to be paid for dearly in the long run, because to some extent it obviated the necessity for measures to restore a balanced economy. What matters from the point of view with which we are here particularly concerned is that, with the aid of efficient European markets to which excessive demand for foreign loans can be diverted, the United States is in a better position to pursue the monetary policy of its choice more effectively.

The practice of issuing Euro-bonds has obviously contributed towards the progress of internationalisation of finance. Issuing centres have acquired the habit of lending in terms of the currency that serves best the purposes of the transactions instead of feeling bound to lending in terms of their own local currency. The existence of the new facilities makes it easier for borrowers to raise capital in the cheapest market and in terms of a currency which suits their purpose. This effect again is the same in the sphere of long-term capital issuing activity as that of the Euro-dollar system in the sphere of international short-term credits. Lenders and borrowers feel no longer tied to transacting business solely in the lenders' currency. Moreover, Euro-bonds, just like Euro-dollar deposits, have a truly international market.

Internationalisation of finance is very far from being an unqualified advantage. An increase in the international character of financial markets means, in given circumstances, an increase in potential instability. The possibility of marketing the Euro-bonds in several centres increases the possibility of hot money movements whenever the dollar comes under a cloud. But, then, anything that makes for a greater freedom in the international movements of funds – or, for that matter, of goods – tends to produce a similar potentially unsettling effect. There can be no safeguard against disturbing international movements of money except through exchange control. And even the advanced controls that existed in Britain in 1949 were unable to prevent a landslide against the pound leading to its devaluation.

International co-operation between issuing houses has long traditions. Centuries before loans came to be raised by means of the public issues practised in our days, transactions were often arranged with the participation of banking houses of more than one country. Before 1914, and again between the wars, international loans were often issued simultaneously in several markets. But on such occasions each issuing house usually operated in its own territory, and the issues were divided into separate local tranches for that purpose. The recently issued dollar, D. mark and unit of account loans, on the other hand, were handled by members of international banking groups without regard to national frontiers. In particular London's share, since it could not be placed in Britain, had to be placed with overseas clients – amongst them investors resident in countries the banks of which were participating in the consortium. To try to place the bonds in another country which is represented on the consortium is no longer considered poaching on other issuing houses' preserves. Underwriting as well as placing of Euro-issues has become thoroughly international in character.

The issue of Euro-bonds by international banking groups and the arrangement of dealing facilities on several Stock Exchanges constitutes an important step in the direction of international co-operation aiming at a better satisfaction of capital requirements.

While between the wars and for a long time since the end of
the second World War sterling was holding its own in its
competition with the dollar for supremacy in the sphere of
international financing, during the middle and late 'sixties
sterling conceded defeat. It is now a generally admitted fact
that the dollar has replaced the pound as the leading international currency. Most refugee funds gravitated towards
New York and they are still held in U.S. dollars with American
banks, though more recent flight moneys preferred Switzerland
and West Germany. Much foreign trade outside the Sterling
Area is now conducted in dollars instead of in sterling. The Euro-
dollar system has given the dollar added significance as an
international currency. Now the use of the dollar as the currency
of most loans issued outside the United States and take up by
investors outside the United States has created additional uses
for dollars, and this tends to create additional demand for them
in the international field.

One of the major defects of the modern financial system,
criticised by the Radcliffe Report and other authoritative
voices, is the absence of adequate channels of communication
between short-term and long-term loans. There can be no
time arbotrage between them. The market in Euro-bonds
provides a possibility for the development of such channels.
As and when Euro-dollar deposits become longer it will become
easier to switch into Euro-bonds and vice versa. It is true,
the two forms of investment are not strictly comparable. Their
security is not identical, and funds invested in dollar bonds can
be realised without awaiting their maturity, though holders may
have to accept a loss. But this difference in liquidity may be
overcome by an escape clause that can be inserted in time
deposit arrangements.

We discussed in Chapter 8 the structure of international
long-term interest rates created by the Euro-bond market.
Should this market expand that structure might well influence
domestic long-term interest rates which would tend to gravitate
towards it. In countries which do not possess a good market
in long-term bonds long-term interest rates are apt to be too

high in spite of the relatively low short-term interest rates. The existence of a rival market might affect the whole structure of domestic long-term interest rates.

A really extensive popularisation of Euro-bonds might induce even financially strong countries to use that market for domestic borrowing, not because the local currency is distrusted by local investors but because interest rates might be lower owing to the international marketability of the bonds. Some Governments of advanced countries, such as Denmark and Norway, have already discarded inhibitions which would have prevented them until recently from issuing their loans in terms of dollars in the domestic market. So long as part of the loans are issued in foreign centres, even though the bulk of it is issued in the local market, they do not feel the transaction is detrimental to the prestige of the national currency.

Thanks to the expanding practice of Euro-bond issues, there has been a strong revival of foreign lending. Before the Wall Street slump the issue of bonds was the main form in which long-term capital was lent abroad, but during the 1930s, the war and the early post-war period it had fallen virtually into disuse. Its place was taken partly by inter-Government loans and partly by direct investment. The former has grave disadvantages as it deprives borrowers of the incentive to achieve creditworthiness. The latter is confined to large industrial firms and provides no facilities for institutional or private investors. The issue of Euro-bonds – whether in dollars, D. marks or units of account – is the answer, and it should go a long way towards facilitating non-official investment abroad which is based more broadly than direct investment, from the point of view of both origin and destination of the funds. The issue of convertible bonds in foreign countries encourages portfolio investment in foreign equities.

The advantages of the emergence and expansion of the Euro-bond market and for issues in other denominations may be summarised as follows:

(1) Advantages to issuing houses and underwriters.

    (a) Earning of commissions.

(*b*) Capital gains (if any).

(*c*) Gaining experience.

(*d*) Gaining additional prestige.

(*e*) Securing additional foreign clients.

(*f*) Earnings by paying agents for the loans.

(2) Advantages to investors.

    (*a*) Possibility of higher yields than on loans issued in New York.

    (*b*) Additional facilities to spread their risk.

    (*c*) Additional facilities to hedge against devaluation.

(3) Advantages to borrowers.

    (*a*) Additional facilities for long-term loans.

    (*b*) Increase of competition by lenders.

    (*c*) Dealing with banks more familiar with their credit-worthiness.

    (*d*) Wider choice of currencies in which to borrow.

(4) Advantages to borrowing countries.

    (*a*) Meeting balance of payments deficits.

    (*b*) Offsetting the outflow of foreign balances.

    (*c*) Stimulating the growth of the economy.

    (*d*) Strengthening the gold and foreign exchange reserve.

    (*e*) Relieving scarcity of credit and capital.

    (*f*) Meeting budgetary deficits.

    (*g*) Consolidating external floating debts.

(5) Advantages to lending countries.

    (*a*) Neutralising unwanted balance of payment surplus.

    (*b*) Diverting unwanted influence of 'hot money'.

    (*c*) Stimulating exports.

    (*d*) Earning invisible exports (commissions etc.).

    (*e*) Securing economic influence in borrowing countries.

    (*f*) Supporting allied and friendly countries.

    (*g*) Developing facilities liable to assist also in domestic capital issues.

(6) Advantages to entrepôt countries.

    (*a*) Earning invisible exports.

    (*b*) Keeping lending mechanism in practice.

    (*c*) Strengthening valuable international connections.

(*d*) Gaining prestige.

(*e*) Stimulating exports.

(*f*) Supporting friendly countries.

There are, admittedly, many items on the other side of the balance sheet. The practice entails disadvantages and risks. But in view of its many advantages there can be little doubt that its adoption has been a welcome step in the right direction.

CHAPTER NINETEEN

Future of the Euro-Bond Market

WHEN working on my book *The Euro-Dollar System* in 1963 I had no hesitation to conclude that the Euro-dollar market had come to stay and that, temporary fluctuations apart, it would continue to expand. When working on the original edition of the present book in 1964 I did not feel justified in being quite so categorical in my forecast of the future of the Euro-bond market. Nevertheless, on balance I was satisfied that the odds are in favour of its establishment of an integral part of the international financial system. In the meantime my opinion about the permanent character of the new market and about the prospects of its further expansion has strengthened considerably. This conclusion rests on the following arguments:

The United States is unlikely ever to assume again so unilaterally the burden of meeting the capital requirements of the free world as she did until 1963. For one thing the coincidence of the circumstances as a result of which a high proportion of the world's financial resources came to accumulate in American hands is not likely to recur, at any rate not in the lifetime of the present generation. The greater part of the monetary gold piled up in Fort Knox has become redistributed and the United States is burdened with an external floating debt amounting to several times its gold reserve. In spite of the simultaneous increase in her long-term capital investments abroad and her unrivalled industrial power, she can no longer be looked upon as a source of unlimited financial assistance, whether in the form of gifts or official loans, or in the form of private loans.

Nor is it ever likely to be the ambition of the United States to monopolise the financial power of the free world. Indeed the policy adopted in 1963 under the pressure of the immediate situation, to encourage a dispersal of international financial activity, is likely to stay. Whatever form the official policy aiming at a diversion of much foreign long-term borrowing from New York may assume – it need not necessarily retain the form of perpetuating the Interest Equalisation Tax – no attempt is ever likely to be made to recapture New York's one-sided lead. In any case the world-wide demand for long-term capital is so heavy that even if all obstacles to long-term lending in New York were removed it would not be able or willing to satisfy the whole of it.

The lesson taught by the experience of the 'sixties is bound to be remembered in Washington. It is now realised that the advantages of too one-sided concentration of the international capital market in New York are liable to be outweighed by its disadvantages. In any case it would take a long series of substantial export surpluses to raise the American gold reserve once more to a level at which the United States authorities could afford to view with indifference sharp declines brought about by overlending abroad.

The facilities of the European capital markets are likely to continue to improve. Fiscal and exchange control handicaps are likely to become reduced in the long run, even if relapses cannot be ruled out. Progress will be made towards the adoption of a higher degree of uniformity in practices and regulations. Above all, in several countries the obstacles to portfolio investment abroad by local residents is likely to be relaxed in the absence of disturbing developments that would necessitate their maintenance and even their reinforcement. A prolonged period of stability would encourage the public to invest in Euro-bonds, especially as in the form of convertible bonds they provide some degree of hedge against inflation.

Although the dollar scares appear to have abated, the possibility that some other currency unit – presumably the D. mark – might replace the dollar, at any rate for some time, as the main currency in which Euro-bonds are issued must be borne in mind. Should discussions of an abandonment of gold parities assume more serious form, most investors would insist on safeguards which could be offered them through issuing most Euro-bonds in composite units of account.

What matters is that the system of Euro-bonds, and the mechanism developed for their issue and subsequent sales, is likely to remain permanent. Perhaps the composite unit of account is the unit of the future. Many debtors and creditors might conceivably come to the conclusion sooner or later – especially under floating exchanges or under some other system which allows for more flexible exchange movements – that it would be well worth while to forgo their chances of benefiting from a change in parities or exchange rates to their advantage for the sake of being safeguarded against losses arising from such changes to their detriment. The main obstacles to a popularisation of composite unit of account issues, the complexity of their formula and the uncertainty of the legal position in practice, are not insurmountable.

We must also consider the remote possibility that sooner or later the United States Government might follow the Swiss example in objecting to the use of the dollar as the currency unit for loans issued abroad. As I pointed out earlier, however, the position of the United States with her vast domestic bond market is totally different from that of Switzerland whose relatively narrow bond market is liable to be affected by the issue of loans outside Switzerland in terms of Swiss francs. The only argument that could possibly be put forward in favour of American policy objecting to such use of the dollar – apart from the possibility of the United States adopting exchange control – is that Euro-bonds offer investment facilities for American capital that has found its way abroad for the purpose of fiscal evasions. Since, however, there are many alternative investment facilities for such capital that argument is hardly likely to be conclusive.

A spectacular recovery of Britain's economic position might strengthen sterling's rôle as one of the leading international currencies as a result of a complete elimination of all exchange control and the accumulation of an impressive gold reserve fed by perennial balance of payments surpluses. Although there is no harm in dreaming about this it would be wishful thinking to regard it as a distinct possibility. It seems probable that in Britain exchange restrictions on capital transactions have come to stay, even if there is a remote possibility of their mitigation. Before Britain can hope to achieve and maintain a really satisfactory balance of payments position and reserve position her trade unions would have to be cured of what has come to be known all over the world as 'the English disease'. Unfortunately, miracles seldom happen in the 20th century. There is, on the other hand, a possibility that workers in all industrial countries might catch the English disease, in which case sterling might cease to be affected by it.

A setback in international capital issuing activity might occur as a result of some international financial crisis. Wholesale defaults by foreign debtors, or a currency chaos comparable to that of the 'thirties would effectively discourage the issue of dollar bonds, as indeed any form of foreign lending, as it did in the 'thirties. Such a setback would be temporary, however, even if it might be of a long duration. Having become familiar with the device of issuing loans in terms of a foreign currency unit, the capital markets would revert to its use, as it would undoubtedly revert to the use of Euro-dollar deposits, as soon as conditions made it possible.

It is possible that the Labour Government might tighten exchange control which would prevent the issue of dollar bonds in London. This would constitute a setback to the international distribution of capital resources. Even though Western European capital markets would continue to operate, in the absence of London's participation their integration into a market big enough to serve as an alternative to New York would become more difficult. But sooner or later Britain is likely to discard economic isolationism and London would be allowed to resume its present rôle as an entrepôt for foreign capital.

Taking everything into consideration it seems to be highly probable, that the Euro-bond system has come to stay and that, temporary ups and downs apart, its application will expand with the expansion of European capital markets. It is possible to envisage the development of really active markets in straight bonds with a large turnover both within each market and between them. A basic condition for such an expansion would be, however, a restoration of confidence in fixed interest-bearing securities in general. Should creeping inflation proceed unhindered and at an accelerating pace, distrust in the maintenance of the purchasing power of the dollar, as that of other currencies, is bound to increase. A growing inflation-consciousness of investors would necessitate the payment of increasingly high interest rates on foreign loans as on domestic loans. Alternatively the issue of dollar bonds for private borrowers might increasingly assume the form of convertible debentures whose equity-content would overcome distrust in the stability of the monetary unit. Indeed the possibility that bond issues might be replaced to a large extent by 'Euro-equity' issues cannot be ruled out. On the other hand, it is conceivable that Governments might issue bonds on which the payment of interest and principal would rise with the cost of living or some other index. No such bonds have been issued abroad so far, but it is a distinct possibility.

However this may be, the formula of Euro-bond issues is fulfilling at the time of writing, and is likely to continue to fulfil, for some time at any rate, a highly important constructive rôle. It has contributed and is likely to continue to contribute towards the expansion of European capital markets in accordance with the basic interests of progress. Its survival and expansion could and should be greatly assisted by improvements aiming at encouraging international lending.

One of such improvements, which is actually in force in the United States and in Germany, is the insurance of foreign investments by the Government against political risk. A liberal definition of the meaning of political risk would greatly encourage long-term lending to countries which need it the most. It is a preferable alternative to continued Government aid in the form of inter-Government loans, because of popular conception, based on experience, that default on debts owed to foreign Governments, or even their outright repudiation, is judged by standards that are fundamentally different from those applied to similar acts committed against private creditors. Even some of the most important Governments repudiated War Debts after the first World War, and after the second World War such debts were virtually wiped out by agreement between the creditors and most debtors.

The worst that can happen to foreign investments guaranteed by the Government of the lending country is that the taxpayer would have to shoulder the burden eventually. If such loans are issued in place of outright gifts or loans by Governments and are defaulted upon eventually the taxpayer would be no worse off, and he even stands a chance that some of the guaranteed debts might not be defaulted upon.

But even Government guarantees are open to objection on the same grounds, though to a less extent, as inter-Government loans, i.e., that the debtor might regard them as semi-political debts which could be defaulted upon as a matter of course. In any case, such guarantees obviate the necessity for borrowers to become creditworthy by building up a reputation for integrity.

The correct remedy lies in the hands of the borrowers. They would inspire confidence among investors by accepting some form of code of behaviour devised for the protection of private investors in foreign countries. The World Bank is actively engaged in devising such a code which would entail undertaking to submit to the World Bank the arbitrage, or at any rate for conciliation any disputes arising between Governments of debtor countries and their creditors. One of the main difficulties is the reluctance of borrowing Governments to apply some such code not only to new loans but also to the existing capital liabilities to foreign countries.

Since creditors depend on the willingness of sovereign States to honour their obligations or to enable their private citizens to honour theirs, no international agreement can possibly safeguard them adequately. But closer co-operation between lending countries to ensure that if a debtor defaulted on its loan from one country it should be blacklisted in all countries would go some way towards reducing the likelihood of default.

It would greatly assist the expansion of foreign bond issues if the Governments, banks and Stock Exchanges in the countries where the bonds are issued made a real effort to achieve a high degree of uniformity of their fiscal provisions, exchange restrictions, Stock Exchange practices, legal procedures, etc. As things are, stock arbitrage entails risks even for firms specialising in some transactions, for there is an ever-present possibility that they might not be sufficiently familiar with the laws and practices applied in foreign markets, or that a change in them might have escaped their attention. Discrepancies between laws and practices may be due to differences in their historical evolution, but in many cases it would not be unduly difficult to strike a compromise for the sake of achieving uniformity.

Another sphere in which there is ample scope for improvement is in respect of the reduction of delays in the delivery of Euro-bonds, by means of clearing arrangements, referred to in Chapter 7. At the time of writing there is actually a clearing institution in operation in Brussels. The main advantage of the clearing is that bonds can be transferred from one account to another without any need for their physical transfer from one institution to another. The larger the number of participants the easier is the settlement of transactions by mere bookkeeping entries.

At the beginning of 1969 an international association of banks and financial houses concerned with the issue of Euro-bonds and with subsequent transactions in them was formed in London. Its object is to establish a code of behaviour in respect of Euro-bond transactions and to use its influence and its expert knowledge to persuade the governments concerned to work out uniform rules concerning such transactions.

But the success of the institutional change represented by the evolution of the Euro-bond market does not depend on technicalities. It depends in the long run on the maintenance of a reasonable degree of political and economic stability and on the absence of advanced monetary instability. Above all, it depends on the maintenance of the trend towards continued internationalisation of trade and finance. A return to economic nationalism would bring to an end the close international co-operation which is at present encouraged by the authorities in most countries by maintaining a reasonable degree of freedom for international movements of capital.

It would be bold to attempt to forecast the future trend in the Euro-bond market. Judging by the experience of the two years, 1967 and 1968, for which alone there is an index compiled by the Kredietbank S.A. Luxembourgeoise, the straight dollar bonds are vulnerable to foreign exchange crises. They reacted sharply to the devaluation of sterling in 1967 and to the gold scare in March 1968. But by the end of 1968 they showed a marked recovery, especially the long-term issues. Both D. mark bonds and unit of account bonds remained remarkably stable. Convertible bonds were firm. They rose 123 per cent during 1967–68, which compares favourably with the advance in Wall Street shown by the Dow Jones Index. The crises of 1969 reacted on both sections of the Euro-bond market, but to a much higher degree on the prices of straight bonds than on those of convertible bonds.

Financial uncertainty is likely to affect straight dollar bonds unfavourably while convertible bonds might benefit by it. On the other hand, should there be an effective deflationary drive it would reverse the conflicting trends.

APPENDIX

Expansion of the Euro-Bond Market

THE following figures, compiled by White Weld & Co., indicate the expansion of new issuing activity in the Euro-bond market during the last five years. No figures or even reliable estimates are available about the turnover in the secondary market. But it seems reasonable to assume that the spectacular expansion of new issues during 1968, indicated by the figures, was accompanied by an at least proportionate increase in the volume of dealings both between banks and their clients and between professional dealers.

The table classifying straight bonds according to their maturity shows a sharp decline in 1968 in the amount of long-term bonds maturing in more than 15 years. Bonds between 11 and 15 years' maturity remained the favourite type.

GROWTH OF THE EURO-BOND ISSUES BY TYPE OF BORROWER
U.S. $ million equivalent

	1964	1965	1966	1967	1968
Central Governments	250·5	212·5	95·1	254·7	224·4
Government Guaranteed and Agencies	171·56	222·0	133·6	380·05	354·65
Municipalities	169·75	60·5	35·0	62·0	116·25
International and European Agencies	133·0	142·5	101·0	155·0	25·0
Industrial Companies Straight	60·0	269·4	470·46	817·7	599·8
Industrial Convertibles and with Warrants	72·5	110·0	242·0	247·0	1,810·0
	857·31	1,016·90	1,077·16	1,916·45	3,130·1

GROWTH OF EURO-BOND ISSUES BY CURRENCY
U.S. $ million equivalent

	1964	1965	1966	1967	1968
Dollars	593·	702·5	837·21	1,716·3	2,361·5
Deutsche marks	236·25	250·0	146·25	148·75	662·5
E.U.A.	10·0		74·1	19·0	28·8
£/DM	18·06	64·4	19·6	20·2	57·0
F.Frs.				12·2	20·3
	857·31	1,016·9	1,077·16	1,916·45	3,130·1

ANALYSIS OF STRAIGHT DEBT EURO-BOND ISSUES
BY MATURITY
(Excluding Convertibles and Issues with Warrants)
U.S. $ million equivalent

Years	1964	1965	1966	1967	1968
0–5	20·0	20·0	183·0	230·0	272·5
6–10	20·0	–	162·06	182·0	86·4
11–15	396·5	471·4	260·60	958·7	876·2
16–upwards	348·31	415·0	229·50	298·75	85·0
	784·81	906·9	835·16	1,669·45	1,320·1

Bibliography

Bank of England Quarterly Review, 'United Kingdom Overseas Portfolio Investment 1960 to 1962', vol. iii, no. 2, June 1963.

BARLOW, E. R., and WENDER, J., *Profits and Losses on Investment Abroad*. New York, 1955.

CAIRNCROSS, A. K., *Home and Foreign Investment, 1870–1913*. Cambridge, 1953.

COLLIN, F., 'Europe's Unit of Account', *The Statist*, 28 February 1964.

Comité chargé d'étudier le financement des investissements, *Rapport présenté au Ministre des Finances et des Affaires Économiques*, Paris, 1963.

Committee on the Working of the Monetary System, *Report* and *Evidence*. London, 1959–60.

DENNING, J. D., 'Capital Movements in the 20th Century', *Lloyds Bank Review*, April 1964.

Economic Research Group, Société Générale de la Banque, 'Capital Markets in Europe'. London, 1966.

Economist, The, 'Where Will all the Borrowers Go?' 8 August 1964.

EINZIG, PAUL, *The Fight for Financial Supremacy*. London, 1931.

— *A Dynamic Theory of Forward Exchange*. London, 1961.

— *The Euro-Dollar System*, 3rd ed. London, 1967.

— 'The European Capital Markets', *The National Banking Review*, June 1964.

— *A Textbook on Foreign Exchange*, 2nd ed. London, 1969.

European Economic Community, 'Development of a European Capital Market.' Brussels, 1966.

Federal Reserve Bank of New York Quarterly Review, 'Recent Innovations in European Capital Markets'. January 1965.

— 'Euro-Bonds: An Emerging International Capital Market'. August 1968.

Federal Reserve Bulletin, U.S. International Transactions: 'U.S. International Transactions: Trends in 1960–67'. April 1968.

FEIS, H., *Europe the World's Banker*. New Haven, 1930.

GENILLARD, ROBERT L., 'The Euro-Bond Market', in *European Capital Market*. Federal Trust for Education and Research. London, 1967.

GUTH, W., 'Die D. Mark als internationale Anleihewehrung', *Zeitschrift für langfristige Finanzierung*. Munich, October 1968.

HELLER, H. ROBERT, 'Borrowers in International Capital Markets', *National Banking Review*, September 1966.

HOBSON, C. K., *The Export of Capital*. London, 1914.

IVERSEN, CARL, *International Capital Movements*. Copenhagen, 1935.

KENEN, PETER R., 'Towards an Atlantic Capital Market', *Lloyds Bank Review*, April 1964.

KINDLEBERGER, CHARLES P., 'European Economic Integration and the Development of a Single Financial Centre for Long-Term Capital', *Weltwirtschaftliches Archiv*, 1963, Heft 2.

LAVINGTON, F., *The English Capital Market*. London, 1921.

LEWIS, C., *America's Stake in International Investment*. Brookings Institute. Washington, 1938.

— *The United States and Foreign Investment Problems*. Washington, 1948.

MCMAHON, CHRISTOPHER, *Sterling in the Sixties*. London, 1964.

MACRAE, NORMAN, *The London Capital Market*. London, 1955.

MADDEN, J. T., and NADLER, MARCUS, *The International Money Market*. London, 1935.

MENSBRUGGHE, JEAN VAN DER, '*Foreign Issues in Europe*', *International Monetary Fund Staff Papers*. July 1964.

MIKESELL, R. F. (ed.), *U.S. Private and Government Investment Abroad*. Oregon, 1962.

MYERS, MARGARET G., *Paris as a Financial Centre*. London, 1936.

Neue Zürcher Zeitung, Finanzzentren der Welt. Zürich, 1959.

NURKSE, R., 'The Problem of International Investment today in the Light of Nineteenth-Century Experience', *Economic Journal*, December 1954.

O.E.C.D. *Committee for Invisible Transactions*. 'Capital Market Study. General Report'. 1967.

RIX, M. S., 'The Premium on U.S. Dollar Securities', *Economic Journal*, December 1950.

Royal Institute of International Affairs, *The Problem of International Investments*. London, 1937.

United Nations, *International Capital Movements during the Inter-War Period*. Lake Success, 1949.

— *The International Flow of Private Capital*, 1946/52. New York, 1953.

— *The International Flow of Private Capital*, 1953–55. New York, 1961.

— *The International Flow of Private Capital*, 1956–58. New York, 1963.

U.S. Treasury, *A Description and Analysis of Certain European Capital Markets*. Joint Economic Committee, U.S. Congress. Washington, 1964.

Index

Time Travelers

Adventures in Archaeology

By Sue Bursztynski

PM Non-Fiction

Sapphire Level 29

U.S. Edition © 2001 Harcourt Achieve Inc.
10801 N. MoPac Expressway
Building #3
Austin, TX 78759
www.harcourtachieve.com

Text © 2001 Cengage Learning Australia Pty Limited
Illustrations © 2001 Cengage Learning Australia Pty Limited
Originally published in Australia by Cengage Learning Australia

6 7 8 9 10 11 12   1957   14 13 12 11 10
4500218901

Text: Sue Bursztynski
Printed in China by 1010 Printing International Ltd

Acknowledgments

Photographs on pp 7, 13, 15, 17, 18, 21, 23, 25, 26, 26, 31 by Liz Alger. Thanks to Geoffrey McSkimming for suggested websites. A big thank you to Professor Matthew Spriggs of the Australian National University for helping out with information about how to become an archaeologist.
Photographs by AAP/AFP IEASM Frank Goddio, p. 31 (top); AAP/Associated Press AP, p. 31 (bottom); Ancient Art & Architecture Collection, p. 10; B. Norman/Ancient Art & Architecture Collection, p. 25; Ronald Sheridan/Ancient Art & Architecture Collection, pp. 13 (top), 20 (left), 21, 27 (bottom), 29 (bottom left and right), front cover (bottom left), and back cover; John P. Stevens/Ancient Art & Architecture Collection, pp. 6, 30 (bottom);
The Art Archive, pp. 19, 20 (right); The Art Archive/British Museum, p. 24, and front cover (bottom centre); The Art Archive/Egyptian Museum Cairo/Dagli Orti, p. 12; The Art Archive/Mireille Vautier, p. 14 (bottom left); Australian Picture Library/Corbis, pp. 1, 8 (centre), 13 (bottom), 14 (bottom right), 22, 23, 27 (top), 28, 30; (c) President & Fellows of Harvard College Peabody Museum, Harvard University, pp. 14 (top), 16; Lucasfilm Ltd/Paramount, courtesy The Kobal Collection, p. 4 (left); Mary Evans Picture Library, pp. 8 (bottom), 9, 11 (top); Mary Evans/Veronique Beranger,
p. 11 (bottom); National Geographic Society, p. 17; Newspix/AFP Photo/RMS Titanic Inc./Discovery Channel, p. 5 (top); Photolibrary.com/James
King-Holmes/SPL, p. 29 (top); N.J. Saunders, pp. 2-3, 4 (right), 32-33, and front cover (top); David Hancock/Skyscans, p. 5 (bottom); Werner Forman Archive/Egyptian Museum, Cairo, p. 8 (top), and front cover (bottom right).

Time Travelers
ISBN 978 0 75 781166 1